ACE YOUR FORCES AND MOTION SCIENCE PROJECT

Titles in the

ACE YOUR PHYSICS SCIENCE PROJECT

series:

Ace Your Forces and Motion Science Project: Great Science Fair Ideas

ISBN-13: 978-0-7660-3222-4
ISBN-10:   0-7660-3222-1

Ace Your Math and Measuring Science Project: Great Science Fair Ideas

ISBN-13: 978-0-7660-3224-8
ISBN-10:   0-7660-3224-8

Ace Your Physical Science Project: Great Science Fair Ideas

ISBN-13: 978-0-7660-3225-5
ISBN-10:   0-7660-3225-6

Ace Your Sports Science Project: Great Science Fair Ideas

ISBN-13: 978-0-7660-3229-3
ISBN-10:   0-7660-3229-9

Ace Your Weather Science Project: Great Science Fair Ideas

ISBN-13: 978-0-7660-3223-1
ISBN-10:   0-7660-3223-X

ACE YOUR FORCES AND MOTION SCIENCE PROJECT

Robert Gardner
and
Madeline Goodstein

GREAT SCIENCE FAIR IDEAS

Enslow Publishers, Inc.
40 Industrial Road
Box 398
Berkeley Heights, NJ 07922
USA

http://www.enslow.com

Library of Congress Cataloging-in-Publication Data

Gardner, Robert, 1929–
    Ace your forces and motion science project : great science fair ideas / Robert Gardner and
      Madeline Goodstein.
      p. cm. — (Ace your physics science project)
    Summary: "Presents several science experiments and project ideas about forces and motion"—
      Provided by publisher.
    Includes bibliographical references and index.
    ISBN-13: 978-0-7660-3222-4
    ISBN-10: 0-7660-3222-1
    1. Force and energy—Experiments—Juvenile literature. 2. Motion—Experiments—Juvenile
      literature. 3. Science projects—Juvenile literature. I. Goodstein, Madeline P. II. Title.
    QC73.4.G369 2010
    531'.6078—dc22

                         2008049778

Printed in the United States of America

10 9 8 7 6 5 4 3 2 1

To Our Readers: We have done our best to make sure all Internet Addresses in this book were active and appropriate when we went to press. However, the author and the publisher have no control over and assume no liability for the material available on those Internet sites or on other Web sites they may link to. Any comments or suggestions can be sent by e-mail to comments@enslow.com or to the address on the back cover.

♻ Enslow Publishers, Inc., is committed to printing our books on recycled paper. The paper in every book contains 10% to 30% post-consumer waste (PCW). The cover board on the outside of each book contains 100% PCW. Our goal is to do our part to help young people and the environment too!

The experiments in this book are a collection of the authors' best experiments, which were previously published by Enslow Publishers, Inc. in *Bicycle Science Projects: Physics on Wheels, Science Fair Success Using Newton's Laws of Motion, Science Project Ideas in the House, Science Projects About Physics in the Home*, and *Science Projects About the Physics of Toys and Games*.

Illustration Credits: Enslow Publishers, Inc., Figures 16–23, 25; Tom LaBaff, Figures 24, 26–31; Stefanie Rowland, Figures 5–10; Stephen F. Delisle, Figures 1–4, 13; Gary Koellhoffer, Crooked Grin Design, Figures 11, 12, 14, 15.

Photo Credits: © bubaone/iStockphoto.com, trophy icons; © Chen Fu Soh/iStockphoto.com, backgrounds; © Loren Winters/Visuals Unlimited, Inc., p. 12; Shutterstock, pp. 3, 34, 74, 104.

Cover Photos: Shutterstock

CONTENTS

CHAPTER 1

The Three Laws of Motion 13

CHAPTER 2

Forces, Buoyancy, Levers, and Balances 35

CHAPTER 3

Pushes, Pulls, and Acceleration 59

◑ *Indicates experiments that offer ideas for science fair projects.*

⊙ *Indicates experiments that offer ideas for science fair projects.*

INTRODUCTION

When you hear the word *science*, do you think of a person in a white lab coat surrounded by beakers of bubbling liquids, specialized lab equipment, and computers? What exactly is science? Maybe you think science is only a subject you learn in school. Science is much more than that.

Science is the study of the things that are all around you, every day. No matter where you are or what you are doing, scientific principles are at work. You do not need special materials or equipment—or even a white lab coat—to be a scientist. Materials commonly found in your home, at school, or at a local store will allow you to become a scientist and pursue an area of interest. By making careful observations and asking questions about how things work, you can begin to design experiments to investigate a variety of questions. You can do science. You probably already have but just did not know it!

Perhaps you are reading this book because you are looking for an idea for a science fair project. Maybe you want to learn about Newton's three laws of motion. This book will provide an opportunity for you to understand the concepts of friction, acceleration, buoyancy, gravity, the Coriolis force, centripetal force, and more. You can have fun working with bowling balls, pendulums, levers, toy cars, rockets, marbles, and bicycles. Doing the experiments will help you learn about the science behind some everyday things.

THE SCIENTIFIC METHOD

All scientists look at the world and try to understand how things work. They make careful observations and conduct research about a question. Different areas of science use different approaches. Depending on the phenomenon being investigated, one method is likely to be more appropriate than another. Designing a new medication for heart disease, studying the spread of an invasive plant species such as purple loosestrife, and finding evidence that there was once water on Mars all require different methods.

Despite the differences, however, all scientists use a similar general approach to do experiments. It is called the scientific method. In some experiments, some or all of the following steps are used: making observations, formulating a question, making a hypothesis (an answer to the question) and a prediction (an if-then statement), designing and conducting an experiment, analyzing results and drawing conclusions, and accepting or rejecting the hypothesis. Scientists then share their findings with others by writing articles that are published in journals. After—and only after—a hypothesis has repeatedly been supported by experiments can it be considered a theory.

You might be wondering how to get an experiment started. When you observe something in the world, you may become curious and come up with a question. Your question can be answered by a well-designed investigation. Your question may also arise from an earlier experiment or from background reading. Once you have a question, you should make a hypothesis. Your hypothesis is a possible answer to the question (what you think will happen). Once you have a hypothesis, it is time to design an experiment.

In some cases, it is appropriate to do a controlled experiment. This means there are two groups treated exactly the same except for the single factor that you are testing. That factor is often called a variable. For example, if you want to investigate whether mass affects acceleration of an object, two toy trucks may be used. One is called the control, and the other is called the experimental. The two trucks should be treated exactly the same. Blocks may be added to the trucks so that the second truck will have twice the known mass of the first. The trucks will be pulled and their accelerations measured in exactly the same way. The variable is mass—it is the thing that changes, and it is the only difference between the two groups.

During the experiment, you will collect data. For example, you might measure acceleration of each of the trucks using an acceler-ometer. By comparing the data collected from the control group with the data collected from the experimental group, you will draw con-clusions. Since the two groups were treated exactly alike except for their masses, an increase in acceleration of the experimental truck would allow you to conclude with confidence that increased acceleration is a result of the one thing that was different: mass.

Two other terms that are often used in scientific experiments are *dependent* and *independent* variables. The dependent variable here is acceleration, because it is the one you measure as an outcome. It may depend upon mass. Mass is the independent variable. It is the thing that the experimenter intentionally changes. After the data is collected, it is analyzed to see whether the hypothesis was true or false. Often, the results of one experiment will lead you to a related question, or they may send you off in a different direction. Whatever the results, there is something to be learned from all scientific experiments.

SCIENCE FAIRS

Many of the experiments in this book may be appropriate for science fair projects. Experiments marked with a symbol (⬤) include a section called Science Fair Project Ideas. The ideas in this section provide suggestions to help you develop your own original science fair project. However, judges at such fairs do not reward projects or experiments that are simply copied from a book. For example, a ball or car rolling down an inclined plane would probably impress the judges more if it were done in a novel or creative way. A better project might involve a carefully performed experiment to find out whether the angle at which a baseball is thrown affects the time it takes to reach home plate. This project would probably receive careful consideration.

Science fair judges tend to reward creative thought and imagination. However, it is difficult to be creative or imaginative unless you are really interested in your project. If you decide to do a project, be sure to choose a topic that appeals to you. Consider, too, your own ability and the cost of materials. Do not pursue a project that you cannot afford.

If you use a project found in this book for a science fair, you will need to find ways to modify or extend it. That should not be difficult because you will probably find that as you do these projects new ideas for experiments will come to mind. These new experiments could make excellent science fair projects, particularly because they spring from your own mind and are interesting to you.

If you decide to enter a science fair and have never done so before, you should read some of the books listed in the Further Reading section. The books that deal specifically with science fairs will provide plenty of helpful hints and lots of useful information that will enable you to avoid the pitfalls that sometimes plague first-time entrants. You will learn how to prepare appealing reports that include charts and graphs, how to set up and display your work, how to present your project, and how to relate to judges and visitors.

SAFETY FIRST

As with many activities, safety is important in science and certain rules apply when conducting experiments. Some of the rules below may seem obvious to you, while others may not, but each is important to follow.

1. Have **an adult** help you whenever the book advises.

2. Wear eye protection and closed toe shoes (rather than sandals) and tie back long hair.

3. Do not eat or drink while doing experiments and never taste substances being used.

4. Do only those experiments that are described in the book or those that have been approved by **a knowledgeable adult**.

5. When doing these experiments, use only nonmercury thermometers, such as those filled with alcohol. The liquid in some thermometers is mercury. It is dangerous to breathe mercury vapor. If you have mercury thermometers, **ask an adult** to take them to a local mercury thermometer exchange location.

6. Never engage in horseplay or play practical jokes.

7. Read through the entire experimental procedure to make sure you understand all instructions. Clear extra items from your work space.

8. At the end of every activity, clean all materials and put them away. Wash your hands thoroughly with soap and water.

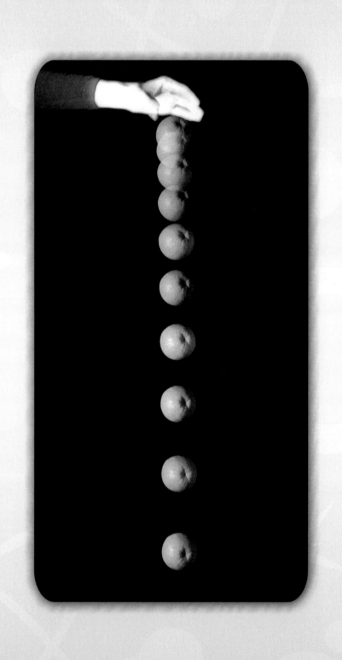

Chapter 1

The Three Laws of Motion

ISAAC NEWTON (1642–1727), ONE OF THE MOST EMINENT SCIENTIFIC INTELLECTUALS OF ALL TIME, WAS THE FOREMOST FOUNDER OF MODERN SCIENCE. He discovered the three laws of motion that present a complete analysis of motion and the rules that govern it. He also stated the law of universal gravitation, which explains the relationships between mass, distance, and gravitational force. Newton founded the sciences of optics and color, explained and predicted the paths of planets and comets, and developed calculus. A poem written by Alexander Pope in the eighteenth century sums up Sir Isaac Newton's accomplishments in these words: "Nature and God's laws lay hid in night; God said, Let Newton be! And all was light."

Newton's three laws of motion were originally published in 1687 in Latin, the language of all scholarly publications in Newton's time. The laws are listed on the next page, both in a modern version and one using everyday examples.

Newton's Three Laws of Motion

First Law: An object at rest will stay at rest and an object in motion will continue in motion at the same speed and in the same direction unless acted upon by another force.

Second Law: The change in speed of an object over a given time is proportional to the force exerted on it.

Third Law: Whenever a force is exerted upon an object, the object exerts an equal force back. This law is often called the law of action and reaction.

Newton's Three Laws of Motion,
Everyday Examples

First Law: When a car stops suddenly, the rider without a seat belt flies forward.

Second Law: A long train is much harder to accelerate than a small car and, once moving, the train is much harder to stop.

Third Law: I would rather collide with a flea than an elephant, especially if they are both moving.

The first of Newton's three laws was built upon discoveries by Galileo Galilei (1564–1642), an Italian experimenter, astronomer, and mathematician. Before the sixteenth century, people thought that it was the nature of moving objects to slow down to a stop. It took Galileo to show otherwise. Galileo experimented with round bronze balls rolling in troughs (a trough is shaped like the gutter in a bowling alley). The ball was allowed to roll down a trough tilted downward and on to upward-tilted troughs (see Figure 1). The smoother the ball and trough, the farther up the ball would roll. However, the ball would never make it back to the starting height. Galileo knew about friction and concluded that if there were no friction, the ball would go all the way back up to the starting height. Note that Galileo could never actually roll the ball without friction. His conclusion was based on a thought experiment; that is, he carried out the final experiment in his imagination.

Galileo also found that if the upward trough was lowered a bit, the ball still rolled almost as high as before; therefore, it rolled a longer upward distance. Lowering the trough more resulted in the ball going an even farther distance. Galileo made a mental leap to the conclusion that if the ball were allowed to roll down to the floor, and if there were no friction to slow it down, it would roll around the world forever. This was a startling theory for his time. The idea that motion would continue unchanged if there was no friction was unique. Galileo's work became the basis for Newton's first law.

Newton built upon Galileo's discovery. He mathematically described the concept of force (a push or a pull). From this he constructed a complete analysis of motion that he was even able to extend to the motion of bodies in the heavens.

In a letter dated February 5, 1676, Newton acknowledged his gratitude to those whose ideas had helped him. He wrote, "If I have seen further it is by standing on the shoulders of Giants."

Have you ever seen an object here on Earth that just kept moving on and on at the same speed in the same direction without anything pushing or pulling it? On Earth, everything always slows down due to friction. To study Newton's three laws, it is advantageous to find a place to carry out experiments with very little friction.

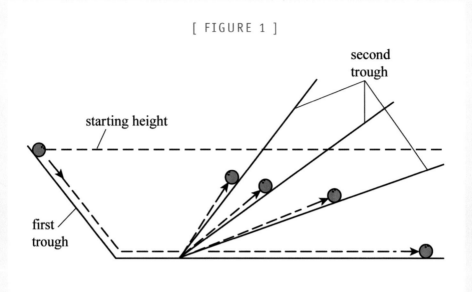

[FIGURE 1]

second
trough

starting height

first
trough

Galileo experimented with balls rolling down one trough and up another.
The diagram shows successive lowering of the second trough. The lower the
second trough, the farther the ball rolled. When the ball rolled a longer
distance, it did not rise as high as before due to the additional friction.
Galileo concluded that a ball that rolled down the first trough onto a
horizontal surface without friction would roll on and on without stopping.

Can you guess one location available to many where this is possible?
Did you guess a bowling alley? All bowling alleys approved by the Ameri-
can Bowling Congress have a very smooth, level surface, most of which is
oiled. The rules say that no area on the bowling lane may be more than
one-tenth of a centimeter (0.04 in) higher or lower than any other
section. The bowling ball must be smooth with the same diameter all
around. All together, these requirements allow a bowling ball to follow a
level, horizontal path on the lane with minimal friction. That is why many
of the experiments in this chapter will take place in a bowling alley.

Each of the three laws of motion will be examined in turn.

1.1 First Law: An Object at Rest or in Motion

Materials:
- smooth floor
- sturdy sheet of paper
- bowling ball or other heavy ball
- drinking glass
- smooth card, such as a card from deck of playing cards
- coin
- 2 marbles of different sizes
- large wok or large shallow mixing bowl

Newton's first law says that an object at rest will stay at rest unless acted upon by an outside force.

Place a sturdy sheet of paper on a smooth floor. Place a bowling ball or any other heavy ball on top of the paper. Firmly grab the two corners of the paper nearest to you. Very rapidly, pull the paper horizontally toward you (see Figure 2). What happens to the bowling ball?

The bowling ball either does not move at all or stirs slightly. The force (pull) acts on the paper but not on the ball. According to Newton's first law, an object stays in place unless a force acts upon it. Since no force acted to move the bowling ball, it stayed in place.

Place a smooth card such as one from a deck of playing cards on top of a drinking glass. Center a coin on top of the card. Then yank the card horizontally off the glass. What do you observe?

[FIGURE 2]

A sheet of paper is yanked out from under a heavy ball. What happens to the ball and how does this illustrate Newton's first law?

The coin falls into the glass. The force of your pull acts upon the card but not on the coin. The coin is left hanging in the air over the glass. The force of gravity pulls it down into the glass.

Newton's first law also says that an object in motion will continue in motion with the same speed and direction as long as it is not acted upon by an outside force.

Obtain two glass marbles of different sizes and a large wok or a mixing bowl of similar shape. Hold the marble against the inside of the wok at the top. Let go of it. Does it roll all the way down and then stop? Does it go partway or all the way to the top of the opposite side? Does it fly out of the wok? Does it roll straight back down again? Try the other marble. Is this result different? Try both marbles several times.

The marble will usually roll to the bottom and almost all the way back up. Then it will roll back down and up the other side but a little lower than before. Then it will roll back down, and so on. The size of the marble does not make any difference in the heights reached.

Since the marble keeps changing direction back and forth, there must be an outside force acting on it. That outside force is gravity. Gravity pulls the marble down, but the marble rolls almost all the way back up each time. It rolls back and forth, in accord with the first law, until friction finally brings it to a halt. Note that this experiment is comparable to Galileo's experiment using two connected troughs.

Materials:

- bowling lane with bumpers in the gutters, or other location with smooth floor

- 6- to 9-lb bowling ball or substitute

- strong smooth wooden plank about 90–120 cm (3–4 ft) long and at least 20 cm (8 in) wide

- several books

- ruler

- pencil

If you do not have access to a bowling alley, you can ask for permission to use another smooth floor such as a school hallway with a vinyl floor or a wooden gym floor. Do not use a carpeted floor; the friction will slow the ball down too much. Instead of a bowling ball, any smooth round ball may be used. The heavier the ball, the better. Please adjust the instructions in this chapter as needed for ball and location.

Before starting, you will need to obtain permission from a bowling alley (or school or other location) to carry out the experiment. Explain that you will be doing a science experiment and using a wooden plank to control the speed of the bowling ball. The plank will not touch the lane itself. Request that bumpers be placed in the gutters on both sides of the lane to prevent the ball from falling into a gutter.

Place a smooth wooden plank on the floor at the foul line pointing down the middle of a lane. Raise the back end 10 cm (4 in) by placing books under it. Mark a line with a pencil about 15 cm (6 in) down from the top of the plank. Hold a bowling ball weighing 6 to 9 lb at the mark (see Figure 3) and release the ball to roll down into the lane. Observe. Does the ball slow down? Does it move in a straight line? Does it make it to the pins?

Lower the back end of the plank to a height of 2 cm (3/4 in) by removing books as needed. Now the ball will not slide down the ramp and along the lane as rapidly as before. Place the ball at the mark and release it. Does the ball make it to the pins? Does it slow down as it moves forward?

Were you surprised to see that, at each speed, the ball rolled along the lane to the very end without a noticeable change in the speed? Even if the ball hit a side bumper, it just kept going. When the plank was barely raised, it probably looked as if the ball would never make it to the pins, but each time it did. Now you know why your little brother's or sister's ball often makes it as far as the pins even when you think the throw seemed too light to ever do it. This is consistent with Newton's first law, which says that the ball will keep moving in a straight line at the same speed as long as no force acts upon it. The frictional force in the lane is very small, so the ball is able to continue moving to the end.

If the ball does not roll in a straight line but curves instead to one of the bumpers, it may be because of the finger holes in the ball. Each time the ball rolls over a hole, you can hear it thump and see the ball slowly shift direction.

Note that for all lanes, there is no oil on the 3 meters (10 ft) of floor in front of the pins. At that point, friction will grab the ball. It will roll, not slide, on in a straight line in the direction that it was going when it came to the unoiled portion. With a good throw, that will produce the sharp "curve" (which is really a straight line) that will carry the ball into the pins.

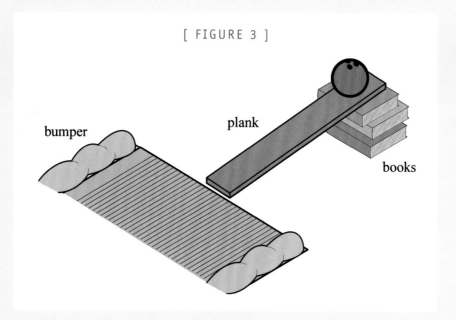

[FIGURE 3]

bumper

plank

books

A bowling ball is allowed to roll straight down a wooden plank onto a bowling lane. The speed of the ball is controlled by propping up the back end of the plank, first with a few books and then with one thin book. Does the ball make it to the end of the lane each time?

Science Fair Project Ideas

- Does a ball on a smooth, horizontal path obey Newton's first law no matter what its weight? Try bowling balls of different weights on the bowling lane and observe what happens. To make a fair comparison, you need to send each ball down the lane with the same force. You can do this by launching all the balls from the same height and angle down the plank. Consider testing other smooth balls such as a billiard ball or a hard rubber ball (always obtain permission to use the different balls on the lanes).

- Does the initial speed of a ball make a difference as to whether the ball obeys Newton's first law? Try different angles of launching to test your hypothesis.

- Construct your own version of Galileo's experiment in which a ball is rolled down a slope and up another one. The two slopes should be close to each other. You may use any ball. Keep a record. What can you do to improve the experiment to get the ball to rise upward to the maximum height? How well do your methods work?

- How did Newton build upon Galileo's work to develop the first law? Investigate and discuss.

- The two greatest geniuses of physics are considered by many to be Isaac Newton and Albert Einstein. Compare their lives and works.

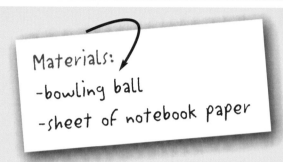

Materials:
-bowling ball
-sheet of notebook paper

Place a bowling ball or other heavy ball on a sheet of notebook paper. Slowly pull the paper toward you. What happens to the ball?

Did you find that when the paper is pulled slowly, both ball and paper move toward you?

Why does this result differ from Experiment 1.1, where the ball stayed in place when the paper was rapidly pulled away? The explanation may be summed up in one word: *friction*.

Friction is a force that arises whenever two surfaces meet, and it always opposes motion. If an object moves forward, friction will slow it down. If the same object moves backward, friction still slows it down.

In the case of the ball on paper, the friction between the ball and the paper holds the ball to the paper unless a greater force than the friction is exerted. This is what happens if the sheet is quickly pulled from under the ball. When the paper is pulled slowly, the smaller force exerted is not enough to overcome the friction between the sheet and ball. They move together when pulled.

Since friction is always involved in motion on our Earth, it is a topic to which this book will return again and again as motion is examined.

Science Fair Project Idea

Compare different surfaces to determine which slows a bowling ball the least, that is, which provides the least amount of friction. For example, try ice, a Formica countertop, asphalt, paper, and others. Also try pieces of the same material that have different degrees of smoothness. How are the results for the same material affected by the smoothness of the surface?

Materials:
- heavy bowling ball
- bowling lane

Newton's second law states that the change in speed of an object over a given time is proportional to the force exerted on it. It may be stated mathematically by the following equation:

Force = mass x acceleration, or $F = ma$

Acceleration is defined as the change in speed of an object divided by the time in which the change takes place.

A bowling ball thrown along an alley will be used to examine Newton's second law of motion. You probably have enough experience with throwing balls to predict that the more force you exert to throw the ball, the faster it will go. This agrees with Newton's second law. As F increases, a also increases (same ball, so the same m). If force decreases, so does the acceleration.

At this point, it is important to recognize that speed and acceleration are not the same thing. Let's look at this by doing an experiment. Be sure to get the permission of the bowling alley manager for this.

Roll the ball down the lane while slapping it onward at intervals with about the same force each time. If you cannot do this at a bowling alley, use an ordinary rubber ball on a smooth floor. What happens?

You will have to chase the ball to keep applying the same force at intervals. The ball should keep going faster and faster. Has the force that you are applying changed? Hopefully, it has not, yet the ball keeps speeding up. How can this be?

The explanation lies in the variable, acceleration. Acceleration measures the change in velocity that takes place over a certain time.

$$\text{Acceleration} = \frac{\text{final velocity} - \text{starting velocity}}{\text{time}}$$

For example, for an object moving in a straight line, the acceleration might be the change in speed in miles per hour that takes place each second. Suppose that the ball was started by a slap that left it going one

Acceleration

mile per hour (one mph). You slap it at the end of one more second to go 2 mph. The acceleration is the difference in speed divided by the time that it takes, so the acceleration is

$$\frac{2 \text{ mph} - 1\text{mph}}{1\text{s}} = \frac{1 \text{ mph}}{\text{s}}$$

Each second that you speed up the ball, you make it go one mph faster than before, so that at the end of 5 seconds, for example, the ball is moving at 5 mph. The same force gives the same acceleration each time, but the speed keeps changing. You have to keep chasing after the ball to keep your hand on it because you are speeding it up all the time with the same acceleration.

You probably also have enough experience with balls to know that the heavier the ball is, the harder it is for you to throw it to get the same acceleration. In other words, the same push given to a billiard ball and a bowling ball will cause the much lighter billiard ball to go much farther.

Science Fair Project Ideas

- Test Newton's second law in another way. Investigate what happens when mass instead of acceleration is your variable. Plan to carry out the experiment with as little friction as possible. A bowling ball on a plank raised at one end can be used to provide the same force each time. Allow the same ball to impact different bowling balls or other balls of different weights. The descending ball must hit each of the others dead center. Measure the change in speed over time for each ball that is hit. Keep in mind that each ball has zero speed when hit. Once the ball is rolling, you can measure its speed (final speed) by finding how long it takes to cover a measured length of the lane. One or more helpers with stopwatches are needed.
  Were you able to verify the mathematical form of the second law? Explain. Construct a graph of mass versus acceleration and explain the shape of the graph.
- Based on Newton's second law, $F = ma$, explain why a bowler would prefer to throw a heavier ball than a lighter one to knock down the pins. Draw a diagram explaining your hypothesis. Find and list other examples of the relationship involved. You might use a bowling ball descending from different heights on a plank to gather data. Report on the outcomes.

Materials:
- bowling lane
- strong, smooth wooden plank, at least 120 cm (4 ft) long and 20 cm (8 in) wide
- gutter in bowling lane
- 4 books, each about 2.5 cm (1 in) thick
- meterstick or yardstick
- pencil
- 4 bowling balls, 2 about the same weight, 1 weighing more, and 1 weighing less

According to Newton's third law, every time a force is exerted on an object, the object exerts an equal force right back.

Newton's third law is, perhaps, the most amazing of the three laws. It may be hard to believe, at first, that every time you exert a force on something, it exerts an equal force back on you. Let's look at how bowling balls act when they hit each other.

As before, obtain permission from the supervisor of a bowling alley or other location before carrying out the following experiment.

Place a smooth wooden plank on the alley floor before the foul line and in line with one of the gutters (the troughs on either side). The gutter will help you to roll balls in line with each other. If you carry out the experiment in a location other than a bowling alley, you will need to place barriers on the floor so that the balls will roll along a straight path. Raise the back end of the plank by placing two books under it. You now have a slope down which to roll a bowling ball into the gutter. Mark a line with a pencil about 15 cm (6 in) from the top of the plank.

Select two bowling balls that weigh about the same. Place one ball in the gutter about 60 cm (2 ft) from the foul line. Hold the other ball at the mark you made on the plank. Let the ball roll down the plank and into the gutter, as shown in Figure 4.

What happens to the ball in the gutter? What happens to the descending ball?

Will the same thing happen if the descending ball moves faster? Place two more books under the plank and allow the ball to roll down the plank to hit the other ball as before. Observe.

In both cases, the descending ball stops when it hits the ball in the gutter. The gutter ball starts moving. When the descending ball goes down faster, the gutter ball moves away faster. This is because the descending ball with the greater acceleration exerts a greater force on the gutter ball.

When the descending ball goes with a higher velocity than before to the point of impact, it goes with a greater acceleration than before. A greater acceleration for the same mass means a greater force. That is why the faster descending ball makes the gutter ball move away faster.

Why does the descending ball stop? Only a force acting upon it could have stopped it. That force could only have come from the ball in the gutter. The force from the ball in the gutter was equal but opposite in direction to the one it experienced.

Did the second ball make it to the pins at the end of the lane? Often, the answer is no. This is because the surface of the gutter is rough. Friction rapidly slows the ball to a halt even though the gutter slants slightly downward.

What do you think will happen if a heavier ball hits a lighter one? What do you predict will happen if a lighter ball hits a heavier one?

Place one of the first two bowling balls into the gutter as before. Hold a heavier ball at the mark on the plank. Release the ball as before. Does the descending ball stop? Does the other ball move?

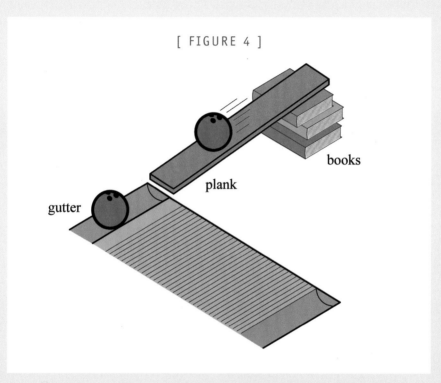

[FIGURE 4]

books

plank

gutter

A bowling ball is shown rolling down a plank into the gutter of a bowling lane. Another ball is in the gutter not far from the plank. The arrangement allows the descending ball to hit the stationary ball in the gutter at its center. Balls of different weights can be placed into the gutter. Each time, the descending ball exerts a force on the ball in the gutter. The ball in the gutter exerts an opposite force on the descending one, according to Newton's third law of motion.

Remove the heavier ball and set it aside. Place the other bowling ball back in the gutter as before. Set the lightest ball on the mark on the plank. Release it. What happens to both balls? How do you explain the results?

When the heavier ball hits the ball in the gutter, the heavier ball slows down but keeps rolling. At the same time, the ball in the gutter (lighter ball) moves rapidly away. To explain this, consider that the third law says that each ball will exert an equal but opposite force on the other one. The first ball, with its larger mass, m_1, exerts a force, labeled as F, when it hits the gutter ball. The gutter ball has a lesser mass, m_2, so it moves off with a greater acceleration, a_2. At the same time, the gutter ball exerts an equal force, F, back on the descending ball. Since the descending ball has a larger mass, m_1, the force, F, is not enough to stop it. The descending ball is slowed but keeps rolling.

action		reaction
$F = m_1 a_1$		$F = m_2 a_2$
heavier ball–O		o–lighter ball
F	$=$	F
since $\quad m_1$	$>$	m_2
a_1	$<$	a_2

When a lighter ball hits a heavier one, the lighter ball moves backward while the heavier one moves forward. This is similarly explained by the third law. The forces are equal and opposite, so the same sized force pushes the heavier one forward but stops the lighter ball and rolls it backward.

Did you ever turn on the water in a hose lying on the ground with its spray nozzle open? The hose probably started to whip around, spraying everything within reach. This was because the squirting water exerted an equal force back on the hose. You can see why such a tremendous, strong concrete pad is needed under a NASA rocket upon launching.

Does the third law mean that when you lean on a wall, the wall is leaning on you? Certainly. Otherwise, you and the wall would fall down.

Science Fair Project Idea

In terms of Newton's third law, show what forces are involved when (1) a bowler picks up a ball, (2) walks (or runs) forward with it, (3) swings it backward, (4) swings it forward, and (5) releases it. Make diagrams to illustrate the equal and opposite forces. Design an experiment that will investigate these forces.

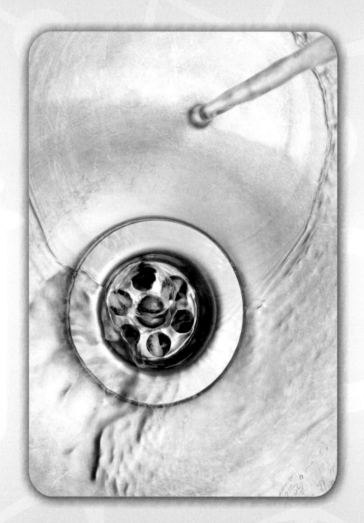

Even your bathtub can come in handy for physics experiments, such as when demonstrating the Coriolis effect in Experiment 2.5.

Chapter 2

Forces, Buoyancy, Levers, and Balances

THE KITCHEN IS AN EXCELLENT PLACE TO DO FORCES AND MOTION EXPERIMENTS. There is usually plenty of counter space, hot and cold running water, a sink, stove, and refrigerator, as well as lots of hardware. A kitchen may also be a busy place, especially before and after meals, so you must be considerate of other people who have to use your "laboratory" for essential tasks.

Although the bathroom is probably one of the smallest rooms in your home, it probably has a bathtub, which offers a large space for doing experiments that require or take place in water. It likely has a sink and counter space. Consequently, a bathroom can serve as a laboratory, but remember that bathrooms are usually shared. Try to do your experiments when the bathroom is not needed by others.

Furthermore, in doing experiments, you may spill water, mess up a sink or counter, or accumulate materials needed to carry out an investigation. If you do, clean up after yourself. Put things away so your experiments do not interfere with the others who need to use this space. Your family will appreciate it if you do; they may be upset with you if you do not. These words of caution to a wise scientist should be sufficient.

Materials:

- spring balance
- small metal object or lump of clay
- thread
- graduated cylinder or metric measuring cup
- water
- container
- balance pan or scale
- notebook and pencil

Archimedes, a Greek physicist who lived in the third century B.C., made discoveries that are as relevant today as they were more than two thousand years ago. You can repeat one of his investigations in your kitchen.

Use a spring balance to weigh a metal object or a lump of clay suspended from a thread. Record its weight in grams in your science notebook. If your spring balance is calibrated in ounces, you can convert ounces to grams— 1 ounce is equal to 28.4 grams.

Then find the volume of the metal or clay by placing it in a graduated cylinder or measuring cup that is partially filled with water. Of course, the level of the water in the graduated cylinder or measuring cup will rise when you add the metal or clay. How can you find the volume of the metal or clay object? Record that volume.

The density of water is 1.0 gram per cubic centimeter (g/cm³) or 28.4 grams per ounce. (A cubic centimeter [cm³] has the same volume as a milliliter [ml].) What weight of water was displaced by the metal or clay object?

Now weigh the metal or clay object while it is submerged in a container of water as shown in Figure 5. How much does the object weigh while suspended in water? What upward (buoyant) force did the water provide the object? How does the buoyant force on the object compare with the weight of the water displaced by the object? The answer to this question was Archimedes' discovery.

Forces

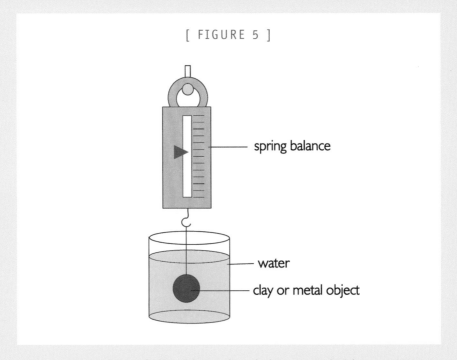

[FIGURE 5]

spring balance

water

clay or metal object

What is the weight of the object when it is suspended in water? How much did it weigh while suspended in air? How does its loss of weight in water compare with the weight of the water it displaces?

Place a container of water on a balance pan or scale. Will the mass of the container increase if you use a thread to suspend a metal or clay object in it? Try it! Were you right? What will be the increase in the mass of the container of water if you drop the metal or clay object into it?

Will the mass of the container increase if you stick your fingers into the water in the container? Try it! Were you right? How do you explain what you observed?

Suppose an object floats in water. It will weigh zero when suspended from a spring scale and lowered into water. How can you find the buoyant force on an object that floats? How can you find its volume?

Materials:
- tall, clear glass bottle or jar with cork or rubber stopper that fits mouth
- water
- glass eyedropper
- condiment packets like those at fast-food restaurants
- jar of water
- plastic soda bottle with screw-on cap

Fill a tall, clear glass bottle or jar almost to the top with water. Draw water into an eyedropper and put the filled eyedropper, pointed end first, into the jar. Adjust the amount of water in the eyedropper so that it just floats. The tip of the rubber bulb should be just above the water level in the jar. Put the cork or rubber stopper in the mouth of the bottle or jar as shown in Figure 6, but do not push it down yet.

Watch the eyedropper as you gently push the stopper into the bottle or jar. What happens to the eyedropper? What happens when you lift your hand from the stopper? Can you make your "submarine" float midway in the water?

What makes your submarine work? Watch the water level in the eyedropper when you push down on the stopper. What happens to it? What happens to the water level in the eyedropper when you remove the stopper? Can you relate the operation of your submarine to Archimedes' discovery?

Buoyancy Affect Submarines?

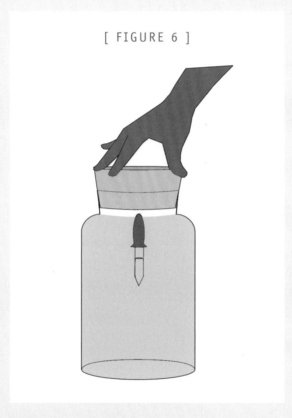

[FIGURE 6]

A miniature submarine can be made from a bottle of water and an eyedropper.

You can make less transparent "submarines" by using squeeze packets that contain ketchup, relish, mustard, or some other condiment. They are found in abundance at fast-food restaurants. To choose the best packet for a submarine, place a few in a jar of water. The best prospect is a packet that barely floats in water.

Push the chosen packet through the mouth of a plastic soda bottle filled with water. Be careful not to break the packet open. Return the screw-on cap to the bottle and your submarine is ready. What happens when you squeeze the bottle? What happens when you stop squeezing? Can you explain how this submarine works?

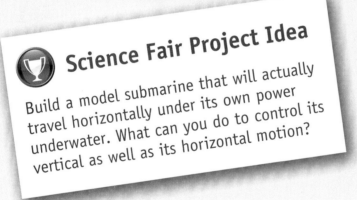

Science Fair Project Idea

Build a model submarine that will actually travel horizontally under its own power underwater. What can you do to control its vertical as well as its horizontal motion?

2.3 How Do Levers and Balances Work?

Materials:
- plastic soda straw
- paper clips
- straight pin
- 2 small identical tin cans or drinking mugs
- felt-tipped pen
- ruler
- partner
- notebook and pencil

Another discovery of Archimedes involved levers and balances. You can learn much about levers and balances with a simple plastic soda straw and some paper clips.

Begin by placing a pin, like the one shown in Figure 7a, across the space between two small identical tin cans or drinking mugs. Can you balance a soda straw by placing it on the pin?

You probably found it impossible to balance the soda straw by placing it on the pin. Perhaps you can balance it if you push the pin through the straw. Try each of the three pin positions shown in Figure 7b. In which position was it easiest to balance the straw? Will the straw remain balanced if you turn it upside down?

Now that you know how to balance the straw, use a felt-tipped pen to make marks at 1-cm (1/2-in) intervals outward along the straw from its center. Make marks on both sides of the straw. Hang a paper clip at the mark closest to one end of the straw as shown in Figure 7c. (If the paper clip slides along the straw, pinch the clip so that it grips the straw slightly.) Where can you hang a second paper clip to balance the straw? Where can you hang two paper clips to make the straw balance?

Figure 7d shows drawings of one side of three different balanced soda straws. There are two paper clips on the other side of each straw. Use two paper clips to find out how the other side of each soda straw looks. Then, in your notebook, make drawings of both sides of the soda straws shown in Figure 7d.

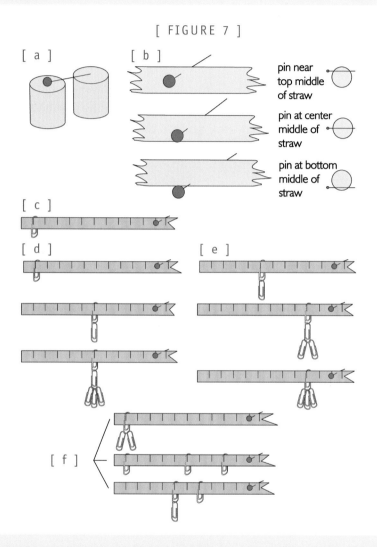

[FIGURE 7]

[a]

[b]

pin near
top middle
of straw

pin at center
middle of
straw

pin at bottom
middle of
straw

[c]

[d]

[e]

[f]

7 a) A pin is placed across two identical supports. b) In which pin position
does the straw balance easiest? c) Hang a paper clip at one end of the straw.
Where can you hang a second paper clip to make the straw balance?
d) Where are the two paper clips on the other side of these balanced straws?
e) Where is the one paper clip on the other side of these balanced straws?
f) Where are the two paper clips on the other side of these balanced straws?

Figure 7e also shows three different balanced soda straws. Only one paper clip is on the other side of each straw. Use a single paper clip on the other side of the straw to make the straws shown in Figure 7e balance. Draw a picture of each balanced straw.

In Figure 7f there are two paper clips on the other side of each straw. Determine the possible positions of the two paper clips experimentally. Then draw pictures of the balanced straws.

Play a balance game with a partner. Place paper clips on one side of the soda straw. Give your partner a certain number of paper clips and challenge him or her to place the clips on the other side of the straw and make it balance without moving the paper clips a second time. Then let your partner challenge you. Can the two of you devise a rule that will allow you to make the straw balance for any situation?

 Science Fair Project Idea

How can you modify your soda straw to make a balance that can be used to weigh small objects? How is this experiment related to a seesaw (teeter-totter) on a playground?

Materials:

- soda straw
- machine screw that fits snugly into the end of the soda straw
- straight pin
- scissors
- ruler
- 2 short tin cans such as tuna fish cans
- small objects such as hair, small pieces of paper or foil, an insect's wing, and others
- clothespin
- file card
- pencil
- laboratory balance (borrowed from your science teacher)
- meterstick or yardstick
- fine wire and wire cutter, or sheet of graph paper and scissors
- forceps (tweezers)
- hair of different colors

You can make a very sensitive balance, one that can weigh very small objects, by using a soda straw that has its point of support close to one end rather than in the middle. To build such a balance, begin by finding a machine screw that fits snugly into the end of a soda straw. Turn the screw until about half of it is in the straw. Find the approximate balance point of the straw and screw by resting it on your finger. Why does it balance close to the end with the screw?

You will stick a pin through the straw above the approximate balance point. As you know from the previous experiment, the pin should be above the midline of the straw. However, to make the balance very sensitive, push the pin through the straw just slightly above the midline. With scissors, cut out about 1 cm (1/2 in) from the top of the straw at the very end of the balance's long arm (see Figure 8). The cut-out section of the straw will serve as your balance pan. It can hold the small things you will weigh. Support the balance by placing the pin on the edges of two short tin cans such as tuna fish cans.

Place some small objects such as a hair, a small piece of paper or foil, an insect's wing, and others, on the balance pan. Does the balance respond to such objects? If it does not, you may need to move the pin to a point slightly closer to the midline of the soda straw.

Use a clothespin to support a file card in a vertical position close to the balance pan. Use a pencil to mark the position of the balance pan (see Figure 8).

To make a scale for your balance so that you can use it to weigh objects in fractions of a gram, you will have to calibrate it. You can do this by first turning the screw at the short end of the balance until the other end of the beam is tipped slightly upward. Then use a standard laboratory balance, such as one at your school, to weigh a 1-m (1-yd) length of fine wire or a sheet of graph paper. Cut off a 1-cm length of the wire or a single square from the graph paper. Assuming the wire or paper is uniform, how much does the short length of wire or the paper square weigh? Use forceps (tweezers) to put the known weight on the

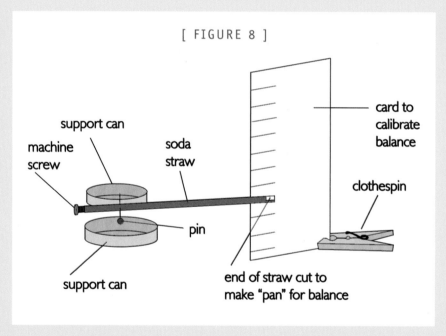

[FIGURE 8]

machine
screw

support can

support can

soda
straw

pin

card to
calibrate
balance

clothespin

end of straw cut to
make "pan" for balance

A sensitive balance can be made from a soda straw.

balance pan. It should tip the end of the balance to a slightly lower but distinctly new position. Mark the new position of the balance pan on the file card and label it with the weight you placed on the pan. If the change in the position of the balance pan is too small to measure, or if the balance pan tips by a large amount, you will have to use larger or smaller lengths of wire, finer wire, or more or fewer squares of graph paper until you find a convenient measuring unit of wire or paper.

Once you find the proper weight to tip the beam by a reasonable amount, you can finish calibrating your balance. Simply place one, two, three, four, and so on, units on the pan and make marks on the card to show where the end of the beam is located when these known weights are on the pan. How can you use the calibrated balance to weigh small objects? How many small objects can you find to weigh? How much does each of them weigh?

You might use your balance to compare the weights of different-colored hairs. Choose a standard length of hair that you can weigh on your balance. Then collect blond, black, brown, and red hairs. Cut them to the standard length you chose and weigh them. Is blond hair always lighter or heavier than black hair?

 Science Fair Project Idea

What other investigations can you carry out with your sensitive balance? Can you find a way to make your balance even more sensitive—that is, to make it respond to even smaller weights?

2.5 What Is the Coriolis

Materials:
- sheet of cardboard
- scissors
- tape
- turntable
- pen or pencil
- sink or bathtub and water

You may have heard that because of the Coriolis force, water always spirals clockwise down a bathtub drain in the Northern Hemisphere and counterclockwise in the Southern Hemisphere. You can test this idea for yourself. Each time you take a bath, watch the water as it goes down the drain. Does it always spiral clockwise?

The Coriolis force or effect, named for the French physicist Gaspard de Coriolis (1792–1843), is a fictitious force that arises because we live on a spinning sphere (Earth). Since Earth rotates once every twenty-four hours, a person on the equator moves through one full circumference (40,000 kilometers or 25,000 miles) in twenty-four hours. This means that person is moving eastward at a speed of

$$\frac{40{,}000 \text{ km}}{24 \text{ h}} = 1{,}667 \text{ km/h (about 1,000 mi/h).}$$

If the same person were standing on the North or South Pole, his or her speed would be zero because he or she is on the axis about which the earth rotates. Someone standing at a point between the equator and one of the Poles moves at a speed somewhat less than the speed at the equator.

A similar effect is true of a disk rotating on a turntable. A point at the center of the disk turns but travels no distance. A point on the edge of the disk travels one full circumference with each rotation. Points between the center and the edge of the disk move at speeds that gradually increase to the maximum speed at the disk's edge.

Now think of a wind moving southward from the earth's North Pole. The wind has no speed to the east. But as it moves south, it flows over land that is moving east (due to the earth's rotation) at ever-increasing speeds. To someone south of the Pole, the wind will appear to move west as well

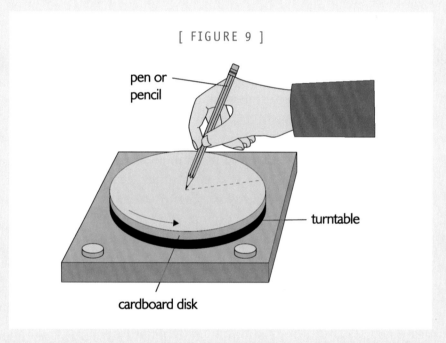

[FIGURE 9]

pen or
pencil

turntable

cardboard disk

What happens when you draw a straight line on a spinning turntable?

as south. Any wind or long-range missile moving due south in the Northern Hemisphere will appear to curve slowly westward, and any wind or missile moving due north will appear to curve slowly eastward.

You can see a two-dimensional "Coriolis effect" by using a turntable. Cut a disk from a piece of cardboard and tape it to a turntable. As the turntable rotates, hold the tip of a pen or pencil at the center of the turntable. Then draw a line straight outward along the cardboard as shown in Figure 9. What does the line actually look like? Is it straight? How can you account for its shape?

If someone is convinced that water always spirals clockwise down a drain in the Northern Hemisphere, partially fill a sink or bathtub with water. Use your hand to give the water a counterclockwise rotation a few minutes before you invite that person to watch the water empty down the drain. Even though the water will appear to be still, there will be enough residual rotation to make the water spiral counterclockwise down the drain. If someone else is convinced that water always spirals counterclockwise, you can demonstrate clockwise rotation by using the same technique.

As you have seen, the Coriolis effect occurs only when a fluid is moving toward or away from the equator. Furthermore, the effect is evident only for objects or masses of water or air that travel long distances over the earth.

Science Fair Project Idea

In the Northern Hemisphere, the plane of swing of a pendulum that swings for a long time, which is what a Foucault pendulum is designed to do, will appear to rotate clockwise. It was probably Foucault's pendulum that led people to believe that water swirls clockwise in the Northern Hemisphere. Using the Internet, find instructions on building a Foucault pendulum like one seen in science museums (or a model of one). Follow the instructions to build your own pendulum and then use it to conduct an experiment.

Materials:
- flexible plastic soda straws
- twist tie
- plastic sandwich bag
- bathtub and water
- food coloring
- long balloon
- aluminum soda can with a pull tab
- string
- nail
- styrofoam coffee cup
- scissors
- thread

In this experiment, you will demonstrate Newton's third law of motion in a bathtub. This law states that if one body exerts a force on another, that second body will exert an equal force in the opposite direction on the first body. When you stand on the ground, you exert a downward force due to the earth's gravity. Newton's law simply says that the earth exerts an equal force upward on you; if you push against a wall, the wall pushes back against you with an equal but oppositely directed force. In these examples, nothing moves.

But suppose you and a friend are standing on a frozen pond wearing ice skates. You place your hands on your friend's back and give a gentle push forward. It is not surprising to see your friend accelerate away from you as you push (an effect of the second law) and then slide away at constant speed once you are no longer in contact. But what happens to you? You, too, accelerate as you push because your friend pushes against you with an equal force in the opposite direction—an effect explained by Newton's third law. And, similarly, you move with a steady speed in the opposite direction once contact is broken.

Of course, the "constant" speed is really not constant. Even on ice there is some friction, and friction always acts against motion. Consequently, you and your friend will eventually come to rest unless you push against the ice with your skates in order to change your motion.

One very simple way to see Newton's third law in action is to let a flexible plastic soda straw hang loosely from your lips. Have the short end of the straw turned at a 90-degree angle as shown in Figure 10a. Blow air into the straw. At the bend in the straw, the straw must push the air to the right or left. The air, in turn, according to Newton's third law, must push back on the straw with an equal but oppositely directed force. What do you see that reveals Newton's law in action?

Now use a twist tie to secure a plastic sandwich bag to the free end of the straw. What happens when you blow through the bent straw with the bag attached? Why doesn't the straw move as it did before?

Fill your bathtub with about 15 cm (6 in) of water. Place a few drops of food coloring in a long balloon. Then fill the balloon with water and place it in the bathtub. Release the neck of the balloon and watch what happens. How is the balloon's motion explained by Newton's third law?

Open an aluminum can with a pull tab. Leave the tab connected to the can. (Do not remove it completely.) Empty the can and attach a string to the tab as close to the can's center as possible. Use a nail to make a hole in the side of the can near the bottom. After inserting the nail, deflect it to one side so that any water in the can will flow out at an angle to the can as shown in Figure 10b. Hold a finger over the hole as you fill the can with water in the bathtub. Then let the can hang from the string as water flows from the can. Which way does the can turn? How is the direction of the can's rotation explained by the third law of motion?

The rotating can is a modified version of Hero's engine. Hero was a Greek engineer who lived in Alexandria during the first century A.D. One of Hero's inventions was a simple steam engine consisting of a hollow sphere with two bent pipes attached to its side. When steam emerged from the pipes, the sphere turned and could be used to do work. Hero had

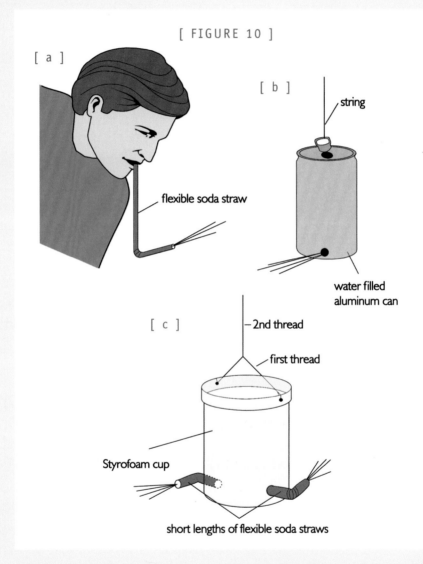

[FIGURE 10]

[a]

flexible soda straw

[b]

string

water filled
aluminum can

[c]

2nd thread

first thread

Styrofoam cup

short lengths of flexible soda straws

Figure 10. These are examples of Newton's third law of motion. a) Blow through a flexible straw that has a 90-degree bend in it. b) Let water emerge at an angle from a can suspended at its top center by a string. c) Let water flow from two soda straws bent at 90-degree angles that open into the lower and opposite sides of a water-filled cup.

discovered an application of Newton's third law long before Newton but never realized the depth or breadth of his discovery.

You can build an engine similar to Hero's that is powered by water rather than by steam. Use a nail to make two small holes near the bottom on opposite sides of a Styrofoam coffee cup. Cut off the long ends of two flexible drinking straws. Push the bent short ends into the holes you made in the cup as shown in Figure 10c. Make two smaller holes on opposite sides close to the top of the cup. Use a piece of thread to connect those two holes and a second thread to suspend the cup as shown so it can turn freely. Fill the cup with water and hold it over your bathtub. How does this modified version of Hero's engine illustrate a practical use of Newton's third law?

What happens if you turn one straw jet around so that the water jets tend to turn the cup in opposite directions? Can you explain why there is little or no rotation of the cup now?

2.7 What Makes a Shower Curtain Move?

Materials:

- an adult
- shower stall or shower in bathtub
- single lightweight shower curtain
- small feather, light strip of plastic, or candle
- alcohol thermometer

Some showers have a heavyweight curtain to avoid the problem you will be investigating. If the shower curtain in your bathroom is heavyweight, **ask an adult** to replace it with a lightweight shower curtain.

As you shower with the light-weight curtain in place, you will probably find that the bottom of the curtain swings inward. Your task is to try to find the force that causes the curtain to move into the shower. Does it happen only when the water is hot? If so, does lowering the water temperature in the shower reduce the amount the curtain moves inward? Does the rate of water flow from the showerhead affect the movement of the curtain?

To investigate the air currents in the shower, you could use a small feather, a light strip of plastic, or, **with permission from an adult**, a candle flame. You might also use a thermometer to measure temperatures at different places in the shower.

Based on your measurements and observations, can you offer a possible explanation (a hypothesis) about why the shower curtain moves inward during your shower? Can you find a way or ways to test your hypothesis?

 ## Science Fair Project Idea

Can you relate this experiment in any way to weather phenomena? Use the Internet to investigate how and why.

2.8 The Transfer of Motion

Materials:
- string
- meterstick or yardstick
- steel washers
- tape
- chair, table, or door frame
- pencil or thin stick

Pendulums are all around us. Watch a hook swinging from a crane. You can determine its length quite accurately by timing its swing. Watch a hanging plant or wind chimes in a breeze. Or watch the slow swing of a giraffe's or an elephant's long legs as it walks. Compare their period (the time it takes the pendulum to make one complete swing, over and back) with the rapid natural motion of a small dog's legs. Compare the gaits of a professional basketball center and a young child.

Hang two pendulums of equal length (about 2 feet), and with equal weight bobs, side by side from a chair, tabletop, or door frame. They should be about 15 cm (6 in) apart (see Figure 11). As you can see, they will swing with the same period.

Connect the two pendulums with a thin stick or pencil. Wind each pendulum's string around the stick once about a foot above the bobs. Pull one bob to the side and let go. Notice how it transfers its motion to the other bob because of their connection.

To make the pendulum do a twisting dance, move the stick down closer to the bobs. What happens now after you start one pendulum?

What happens if you change the weight of one bob by adding more washers?

[FIGURE 11]

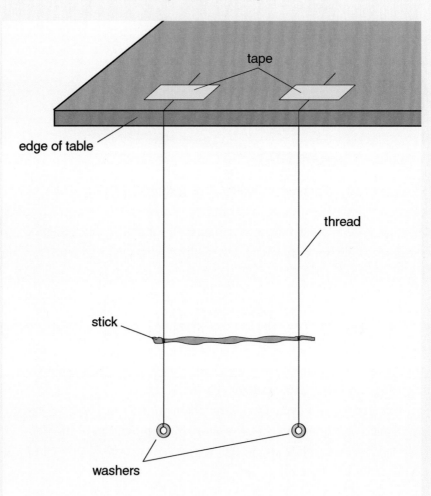

Pushes, Pulls, and Acceleration

IF YOU SAW A BOOK BEGIN TO SLIDE ALONG A TABLE WITHOUT BEING PUSHED, OR A BALL BEGIN TO BOUNCE WITHOUT HAVING FALLEN, YOU MIGHT THINK POLTERGEISTS WERE AT WORK. Certainly something unnatural would be happening. But why would you think so?

Sir Isaac Newton provided the answer more than three hundred years ago. He realized that objects move only when forces (pushes and pulls) are applied. He also noticed that when a force acts on an object, that object accelerates positively or negatively (speeds up or slows down). Sometimes accelerations are not easy to detect. In order to better understand acceleration, you may build an accelerometer. It will indicate the direction of the acceleration as well as its presence.

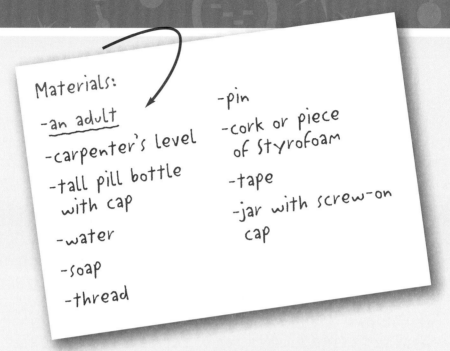

Materials:

-an adult
-carpenter's level
-tall pill bottle
 with cap
-water
-soap
-thread

-pin
-cork or piece
 of Styrofoam
-tape
-jar with screw-on
 cap

You can use a small carpenter's level as an accelerometer, or you can build something similar by filling a tall pill bottle with water (see Figure 12). Leave a little space at the top so there will be a bubble when you put the cap on. A tiny piece of soap in the bottle will prevent the bubble in your bubble accelerometer from sticking to the sides of the bottle.

To build a cork accelerometer, tie a piece of thread to the head of a straight pin (see Figure 12). Stick the pin into a small cork or a piece of Styrofoam. Tape the free end of the thread to the center of the screw-on cap of a clear glass or plastic jar. Fill the jar completely with water, screw on the cap, and invert the jar. Presto! You have an accelerometer.

Place an accelerometer on a countertop and move it gently back and forth. Watch what happens when you start or stop moving the accelerometer. Notice that the cork or bubble moves in the direction of the acceleration. The acceleration is always in the direction of the force—with the motion to start, against the motion to stop. In order to stop a body, the force has to oppose the motion. The acceleration must be negative; that is, there must be a decrease in speed.

[FIGURE 12]

BUBBLE ACCELEROMETER

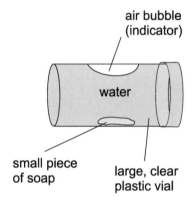

air bubble
(indicator)

water

small piece
of soap

large, clear
plastic vial

CORK ACCELEROMETER

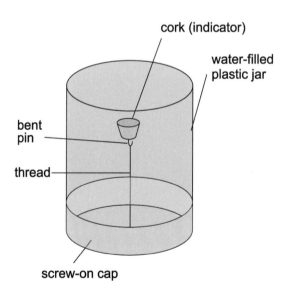

cork (indicator)

water-filled
plastic jar

bent
pin

thread

screw-on cap

Take an accelerometer on a walk. Be sure to keep it level. Do you accelerate as you walk?

Ask an adult to take you for an automobile ride. Bring your accelerometer along. Can it detect accelerations in the car? Do any of the directions surprise you?

Science Fair Project Idea

Design and carry out an experiment using your accelerometer.

3.2 What Happens to Acceleration as the Force Increases?

Materials:

- accelerometer (made in Experiment 3.1)
- fairly heavy toy truck or small wagon
- identical rubber bands or sensitive spring scale
- ruler

Mount an accelerometer on a toy truck or a small wagon. Attach a rubber band or a spring scale to the front of the truck or wagon. How big a stretch is needed to make the vehicle move along with a slow but constant speed? This is the minimum force needed to overcome friction. (You can measure the stretch on a rubber band by placing it above a ruler as you pull it.)

Pull the toy again. This time stretch the rubber band more than enough to overcome friction. Keep the rubber band stretched the same amount as you pull. What happens to the truck's or wagon's speed as you pull? What does your accelerometer indicate?

Repeat these steps, but double the force by stretching *two* side-by-side rubber bands as much as you stretched one before. What happens to the acceleration as the force gets bigger?

3.3 How Does Adding Weight Affect Acceleration?

Materials:
- materials from Experiment 3.2
- some weights to add to the truck or wagon

What do you think will happen to the acceleration of your truck or wagon if you add more weight to it without changing the force?

Test your prediction by first accelerating the vehicle with a certain force. Then add weight so that the amount of matter is at least doubled. Repeat the experiment using the same force. What happens to the acceleration of the truck? Were you right?

3.4 How Does the Speed of Spinning Objects Affect Acceleration?

Materials:
- accelerometer (made in Experiment 3.1)
- turntable or lazy Susan
- cardboard
- scissors
- clear tape
- marking pen

You probably were not surprised to find that heavy things move more sluggishly than lighter ones given the same force. Nor were you startled to learn that bigger forces give bigger accelerations. After all, you know that you can accelerate a tennis ball a lot more easily than a bowling ball, and that a tennis ball will attain greater speed if you hit it harder.

The interesting thing is that Newton used this simple under-standing of force and acceleration to explain the movement of the planets and stars as well as that of falling bodies and horse-drawn carriages. In fact, he used it to explain all motion.

But planets move about the sun in near circles with nearly constant speed. Can a force be acting on them if they are moving at constant speed?

You can do a simple experiment to find out. Hold an accelerometer at arm's length (be sure it is level) and turn around, watching the accelerometer as you turn. What do you find?

To see what is happening in more detail, tape an accelerometer to a turntable or lazy Susan. When the table turns at a steady speed, is there an acceleration?

Were you surprised? What was the direction of the acceleration? What must have been the direction of the force?

To see if the acceleration is related to the speed, change the speed of the turntable, or move the accelerometer closer to and then farther from the center of the spinning table. Where is the speed of a spinning table greatest? Where is its speed zero?

How is the acceleration affected by the speed?

See if you can predict the direction of the acceleration on a playground merry-go-round, a toy train moving along a circular track, or a car rounding a curve.

By the way, have you ever tried to draw a straight line on a spinning turntable?

Cut a piece of cardboard to fit the turntable and fasten it on with tape.

Can you figure out a way to draw a circle on a spinning table? It is really very easy. But try to draw a straight line from the center to the edge of the table while it is turning.

Not so easy, is it? Can you figure out a way to do it? (*Hint:* How does the speed of any point on the table change as you move outward from the center?)

3.5 What Is Centripetal Force?

Newton knew that an inward acceleration indicated an inward force. He also realized that a force was needed to change the *direction* of a circling body's motion. After all, a change in direction is as significant as a change in speed.

The inward force causing something to move in a circle is called a centripetal force. You can feel such a force by doing the following experiment.

Fill a plastic pail about one-fourth full of water. Take it outdoors or someplace where you can swing it without hitting anything or having to worry about spilling.

Swing the pail in a *vertical* circle that extends from over your head to very near the ground, as shown in Figure 13. (Do not worry; the water will stay in the pail.) You will feel the force your arm exerts to keep the pail moving in a circle.

From what you already know about acceleration in circular motion, would you expect the required force to increase or decrease if you swung the pail faster? Try it. Were you right?

If you add more water to the pail, will the force needed for circular motion at the same speed be greater, less, or the same? Try it.

Why do you think water stays in the pail even while it is upside down? (*Hint:* Suppose the centripetal acceleration of the pail is greater than the acceleration due to gravity.)

Perhaps you have gone through a loop-the-loop on a roller coaster. If you have, then you know what it is like to be the water in the pail.

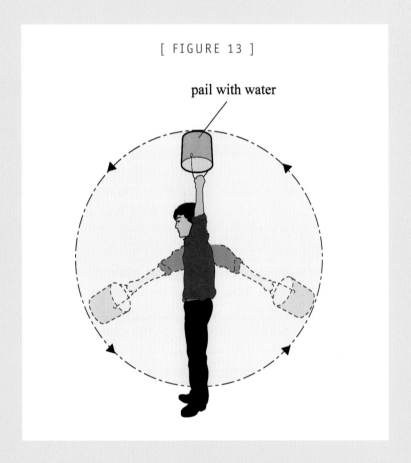

[FIGURE 13]

pail with water

Science Fair Project Ideas

- What is the difference between a centripetal force and a centrifugal force? Why is a centrifugal force often called a "fictitious" force?
- Watch a roller coaster that does a loop. Make some estimates to determine the radius of the loop and the speed of the car that carries passengers. From your estimates, determine the centripetal acceleration of the car at the top of the loop. How does the car's centripetal acceleration compare with the acceleration due to gravity?

3.6 How to Build a Rocket Boat

Materials:
- water
- sink or bathtub
- long balloon
- milk carton
- scissors
- nail

A rocket is an example of the push/push back law. You can make a "rocket boat" as shown in Figure 14.

Cut a milk carton in half the long way to make a "boat". Using a nail, make a hole in the back of the boat. Inflate a long balloon and keep it closed with your fingers as you pull the mouth of the balloon through the hole. Make sure the hole is small enough so that the "fuel" will last for several seconds. What happens when you release the rocket? How does the rocket demonstrate Newton's third law of motion?

[FIGURE 14]

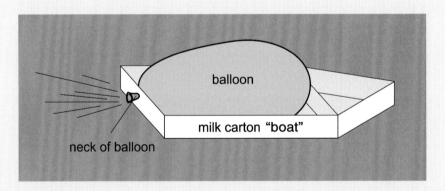

balloon

milk carton "boat"

neck of balloon

Materials:

- wooden blocks
- smooth board
- washers
- weights
- thread
- paper clips
- aluminum foil
- newspaper
- tape
- waxed paper
- construction paper
- thumbtacks
- rubber bands
- round pencils
- ruler

In most of your experiments so far, you have kept frictional forces small by using cars on wheels, marbles, and motions in air. But in most normal activities friction plays an important, often vital, part. Imagine what it would be like to try to walk without friction between your feet and the floor or ground. Imagine how useless cars, buses, and trains would be without friction.

Galileo and Newton were able to understand motion better than others because they could understand what motion would be like *without* friction. But they both knew that friction was a force that always acted against motion. You saw what frictionless motion is like when you rolled balls in a bowling alley (Chapter 1).

Friction is always present when one surface moves over another. But you have probably noticed that frictional forces vary with different kinds of surfaces. For example, it is much easier to walk over a rubber mat than over a polished floor or an icy sidewalk.

[FIGURE 15]

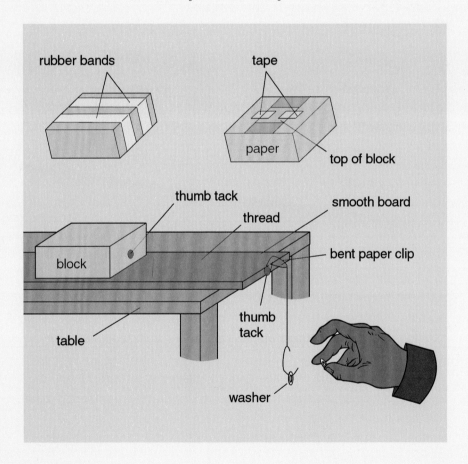

You can use the simple friction tester shown in Figure 15 to measure the friction between surfaces. Place a block on a smooth board and add washers to the hook until the block slides with a steady speed. The number of washers required to move the block is a measure of the friction opposing the motion.

Does it take more washers to make the block begin to move than it does to keep it moving once started?

If you find starting friction greater than the friction present once the block is in motion, try tapping the board as you add washers to free the block.

Is friction related to weight? To find out, put a second, identical block on the first one, or add weights equal to the weight of the block. Is the friction greater? Is it twice as great?

Does the area of the surfaces rubbing together affect friction? If the block is smooth on all sides, turn it so that it rests on a narrower side and see if it changes the number of washers you must add to make the block slide. If the block is not as smooth on its narrow side, cover it with a smooth material—newspaper, for instance—then test the effect of changing the area. What do you find?

Tape a sheet of newspaper to the block. How many washers are needed to make the block slide now?

Repeat the experiment but cover the bottom of the block with aluminum foil, waxed paper, or construction paper. You can put wide rubber bands around the block to make a rubber surface. You can also change the surface of the board by taping various things such as aluminum foil to it. You can test to see the effect of putting the block on rollers (round pencils work well). Try a variety of surfaces and keep a record of your results. What pair of surfaces provides the most friction? Which provides the least?

Another way to test friction is to raise the board as you tap it. Raise one end of the board until the block slides. Then measure the height you lifted the board or the angle it makes with the tabletop. Do your results on this test agree with those of your earlier experiment?

forces on Toy Cars and Trucks

THE NEXT TIME YOU GO TO A TOY STORE, LOOK AT THE GREAT VARIETY OF TOY CARS AND TRUCKS THAT YOU CAN FIND ON THE SHELVES. In this chapter, you will see how some of these toy vehicles can be used in a variety of science experiments. The experiments will involve the effect of gravity on cars, friction, brakes, making cars do loop-the-loops, collisions, safety belts, and lots more. You will be doing a lot of experimenting. Keep your science notebook handy to record your results.

Materials:
- track 60-90 cm (2-3 ft) long (Darda®, Hot Wheels®, and Majorette® make tracks, or you can make your own from cardboard and fold up the sides so the car will not fall off)
- long, smooth, level surface
- several Hot Wheels®, Matchbox®, or similar small toy cars
- 3 identical toy blocks or books
- meterstick, yardstick, or tape measure
- balance or scale
- clay
- shorter or longer piece of track

In this experiment, you will use toy cars and a length of track to investigate how the height and length of the hill affect the distance a car will coast.

Place one end of a length of track 60 to 90 cm (2 to 3 ft) on a block or book, as shown in Figure 16. The lower end of the track should rest on a long, smooth, level surface so that a toy car can travel as far as it will go after rolling down the "hill" made by the track.

Start a toy car from the very top of the track. Let it roll down the hill and along the level surface until it stops. Use a meterstick, yardstick, or tape measure to find out how far the car traveled after it reached the bottom of the ramp. Repeat the experiment four or five times and record the average distance in your science notebook.

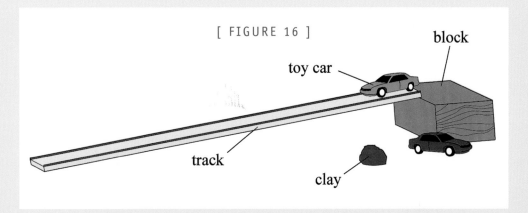

[FIGURE 16]

block

toy car

track

clay

How far will the car go after it rolls down the incline?

Now try another car and measure the average distance it travels over four or five runs. Does it go the same distance as the first car, farther, or not as far?

Predict what will happen to the distance a car travels if you place the end of the track on two blocks or books instead of one. Then make several runs with one of the toy cars. Were you right? Did the car travel twice as far, the same distance, or not as far?

Predict the distance a car will travel when you place the end of the ramp on three blocks or books. Test your prediction. Were you right? Record the results of these experiments.

WEIGHT AND DISTANCE

Do you think the weight of a car will affect the distance it travels after rolling down the hill? To find out, weigh one of the cars on a balance or a scale. Then prepare a lump of clay that has the same weight.

Let the car roll down the track several times and find the average distance it travels. Then hold the car in one hand so that no pressure is applied to the wheels as you gently press the lump of clay onto the top of the car with your other hand. You have now doubled the car's weight. Does the added weight affect the distance the car travels after rolling down the ramp? If it does, how does it affect it?

LENGTH OF INCLINE AND DISTANCE

Do you think the length of the ramp will affect the distance the car travels after rolling down the hill? To find out, measure the average distance the car travels beyond the ramp you have been using. Then test the same car several times on a ramp that is shorter or longer. Does the length of the ramp affect the distance the car travels after it reaches the end of the track? Can you explain why? Design and carry out an experiment to test your explanation.

Science Fair Project Idea

Do real cars on hills behave in the same way that the toy cars did in this experiment? Design experiments to find out. Then, **ask an adult** to drive a car while you carry out your experiments.

4.2 Marbles and Balls on Hills

Materials:
- track 60–90 cm (2–3 ft) long (similar to the one used in Experiment 4.1)
- long, smooth, level surface
- 3 identical blocks or books
- meterstick, yardstick, or tape measure
- marbles of the same and different diameters
- balls such as tennis, baseball, golf, croquet, Ping-Pong, and rubber

In the previous experiment, you found out how far toy cars travel after rolling down an incline. You can use much of the equipment you used in that experiment to investigate how far different spheres will travel after rolling down an incline.

Place one end of a length of track 60 to 90 cm (2 to 3 ft) on a block or book. The lower end of the track should rest on a long, smooth, level surface so that a marble will travel as far as it will go after rolling down the track.

Start a marble from the very top of the track. Let it roll down the hill and along the level surface until it stops. Use a meterstick, yardstick, or tape measure to find out how far it traveled after it reached the bottom of the ramp. Repeat the experiment four or five times and record the average distance in your science notebook.

Now try another marble of the same diameter and measure the distance it travels over four or five runs. Does it go the same distance as the first one, farther, or not as far?

Predict what will happen to the distance the marble travels after rolling down a track when the end of the track is on two blocks or books instead of one. Then try it several times. Were you right?

Predict the distance the marble will travel when you place the end of the ramp on three blocks or books. Test your prediction. Were you right?

Do you think the marble's weight will affect the distance it travels after rolling down the hill? To find out, repeat the experiment with a larger marble. What do you find? Does the weight of the marble affect the distance it travels? If it does, how do you know it was not caused by the size rather than the weight of the marble? Design and carry out an experiment to find out.

Now try some other spheres. Which do you think will roll farther after leaving the ramp, a baseball or a marble? How about a golf ball? a Ping-Pong ball? a tennis ball? a croquet ball? Other balls? Of all the spheres you tested, which one traveled the farthest after leaving the ramp? Can you explain why it traveled farther than the others?

Materials:
-large toy truck
-spring scale or long rubber band
-smooth board about 1 m (3 ft) long
-blocks or books
-ruler

Hang a large toy truck from a spring scale or a long rubber band. Although the rubber band cannot measure weight, measuring the length of the rubber band will allow you to compare weights.

Place blocks under one end of a smooth board about 1 m (3 ft) long. The raised end of the incline should be about 30 cm (1 ft) above the floor (see Figure 17).

Place the truck at the top of the inclined board. Use a spring scale or rubber band to measure (or compare) the force with which gravity pulls the truck down the incline. Record your results. Is the force more, less, or the same as the truck's weight that you measured before?

Now use more blocks to raise the end of the board so it is about 60 cm (2 ft) high. Again, use the spring scale or rubber band to measure (or compare) the force with which gravity pulls the truck down the incline. Is the force more or less than it was when the board was less steep? What will the force be when the incline is at an angle of 90°— that is, when it is vertical? Measure (or compare) the force. Were you right?

Again, place the board so that one end of the incline is 30 cm (1 ft) higher than the end on the floor. How much force is needed to pull the truck along the incline? How much force is needed to lift the truck straight up from the floor to the top of the incline?

Does an inclined plane make it easier to move an object upward? Why?

Turn the truck upside down so that its top rather than its wheels are on the incline. What force is required to drag the truck up the

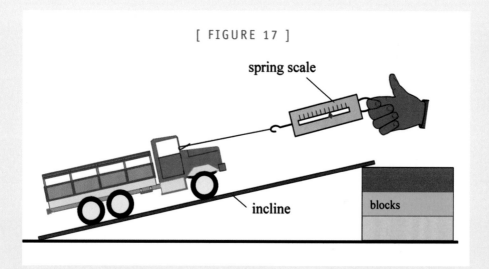

[FIGURE 17]

spring scale

incline

blocks

How does the force of gravity along the incline compare with the weight of the truck when it is pulled vertically by gravity?

incline now? How does the force needed to pull the upside-down truck up the incline compare with the force needed to pull the truck on wheels up the incline? How can you account for the difference in the force needed to move the truck under these different conditions?

Science Fair Project Ideas

- If you slide down a snowy hill on a sled, does the weight on the sled affect the distance it travels after reaching the bottom of the hill?

    The force needed to roll an object up an incline is less than the force needed to lift it straight up to the same height. But do you do less work when you roll an object up an incline than you do when you lift it? To answer this question, you need to first investigate how work is defined in science. Then you can measure work under the different conditions.

- Why do you think engineers define the screw as an inclined plane? Find two screws that have the same diameter but a different number of threads per centimeter or inch. Which screw do you think will be easier to turn with a screwdriver? Why?

- Make a list of the places where you see inclined planes being used. Try to explain why they are used at each site you observe.

Materials:

- loop-the-loop track (from Darda®, Hot Wheels®, or other source)
- toy cars such as Lego®, Hot Wheels®, Matchbox®, etc.
- rulers, meterstick, or yardstick
- spheres such as marbles, and small balls—rubber, golf, and Ping-Pong
- calculator that can find square roots
- electric toy car

Construct a loop-the-loop to which you can attach a straight length of track. It should be possible to raise the end of the straight track well above the highest point of the loop (see Figure 18).

As you may know, an object that is raised to a height above the ground or floor has gravitational potential energy. It can do work if it falls back to the floor. If a ball rolls down an incline shaped like a roller coaster track, the potential energy is converted to kinetic energy (the energy associated with motion). Theoretically, the ball should reach the same height from which it started if it rolls up a similar incline after reaching the bottom of the incline it rolled down. Of course, it never does because it loses some energy due to friction between the ball and the incline on which it rolls.

If you let a toy car roll down an incline like the one shown in Figure 18, at what height (h) must you release the car before it can successfully complete the loop-the-loop? Is the release height required for the car to complete the loop-the-loop the same for all cars? If not, what might cause any differences in the required release height?

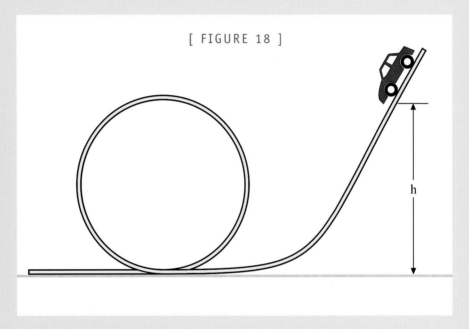

[FIGURE 18]

Small toy cars and balls can roll down the track and do a loop-the-loop.
What is the minimum height, *h*, required for a car or ball to make it
around the loop-the-loop?

Repeat the experiment using a variety of spheres, such as marbles and small balls—rubber, golf, and Ping-Pong. From what height does each sphere have to be released in order to make it around the loop? Do the various spheres differ in the height from which they must be released in order to make it around the loop? If they do, can you explain why?

It can be shown that theoretically there is a minimum height from which an object must be released to complete the loop. That theoretical height, as measured from the top of the loop, is one-fourth the diameter of the loop.

Measure the diameter of the loop-the-loop and then add one-fourth of that diameter. The sum of those two numbers should give you the minimum theoretical height from which an object must be released to make it around the loop. By how much did each of the cars and spheres you tested exceed the theoretical minimum height?

ELECTRIC CARS ON THE LOOP

Many Darda®, Hot Wheels®, and other loop-the-loop tracks include a small toy car with a rechargeable motor. After charging the motor, the car will follow a track that includes one or more loop-the-loops.

The directions that come with the toy may tell you to charge the car's electric motor for a specific length of time, such as 10 seconds. Usually, the specified time will charge the motor enough to make it go around the track several times.

For how long must you charge the car's motor so that it will go around a single loop-the-loop just once?

As you can see, the car with a minimally charged motor moves slower than one that is fully charged. But how fast does it move? What is the approximate minimum speed for a car to make it around the loop-the-loop?

Theoretically, the minimum speed required for the car to make it around the loop is approximately the square root of 5 m/s^2 times the diameter (D) of the loop, that is:

V = minimum velocity; m/s = minimum speed in meters per second; D = diameter of the loop.

$V(\text{minimum}) = \sqrt{(5 \text{ m/s}^2 \text{ x } D)}.$

For example, if the loop has a diameter of 0.3 m (30 cm), the theoretical minimum speed required for the car to make it around the loop is

$\sqrt{5 \text{ m/s}^2 \text{ x } 0.3 \text{ m}} = 1.2 \text{ m/s}.$

Design your own experiment to measure the minimum speed required for the car to make it around the loop. How does the speed you measure compare with the theoretical minimum speed?

Science Fair Project Ideas

- Work out why the minimum height for an object to complete the loop-the-loop as measured from the bottom of the loop is 1.25 times the diameter of the loop.
- Work out why the minimum speed for a car to make it around a loop-the-loop is approximately the square root of 5 m/s² x the diameter of the loop.

Materials:

-toy car or truck 10 cm [4 in] or more in length with wheels that turn freely

-long, wide, smooth board

-rubber bands

Find a good-size toy car or truck with wheels that turn freely. Place the toy car or truck at one end of a long, wide, smooth board. Slowly lift one end of the board until the vehicle starts to roll. What is the slope of the incline when it starts to roll (see Figure 19)? What does this tell you about the friction between the truck wheels and the board?

In the early 1900s, when cars were just beginning to replace horses, some of the cars had brakes on only one pair of wheels. Do you think the brakes were on the front or rear wheels? After you carry out this experiment, you should be able to answer this question.

Place the toy vehicle on the board again. Lift the board a little and the truck will roll straight down. Wrap a rubber band around both the front and rear wheels so that none of the wheels can turn. Will the car roll down the hill now? Will it slide down the hill if you make the hill steeper? How does the friction between the board and locked wheels compare to the friction between the board and wheels that are free to turn? How do you know?

Now, use a rubber band to prevent only the rear wheels of the car from turning. Leave the front wheels free to turn. Again, raise one end of the board until the car starts to slide. What happens to the car as it slides down the hill? Repeat the experiment, but this time use the rubber band on the front wheels only, leaving the rear wheels free to turn.

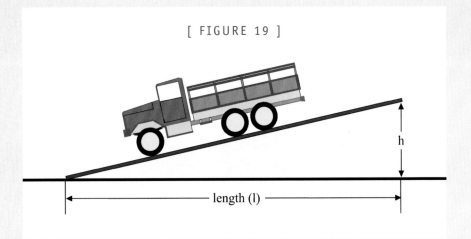

[FIGURE 19]

length (l)

h

The slope of an incline is the height, *h*, to which one end is raised divided by the length of the incline, *l*. If *h* is 5 cm and *l* is 50 cm, the slope is 5 ÷ 50 = 0.1 (1/10).

What happens when the car slides this time? Do you think the front or the rear brakes on a car lock first when a driver steps on the brake pedal? On old cars that had brakes on only one pair of wheels, which pair, front or rear, had brakes?

 Science Fair Project Idea

Explain why the brakes on the front wheels of cars are made to take hold before the rear wheels.

Materials:

- 2 identical toy cars—Lego®, Hot Wheels®, Matchbox®, or similar toy cars
- tape or rubber bands
- 4 or more rubberized or ceramic square or disk magnets (can be purchased at an electronics store)
- 90-cm (3-ft) or longer piece of straight plastic track, such as those made by Darda®, Hot Wheels®, or Majorette®
- balance
- clay
- ruler

Find two small identical toy cars that have wheels with little friction. Use tape or rubber bands to fasten a rubberized or ceramic magnet to the front or rear of each car. Before you fasten a magnet to the second car, be sure the magnet is turned so that it will repel the magnet on the first car. Use a balance to weigh the cars. Their weights should be very nearly the same. If they are not, add a little clay to the lighter car until their weights are equal.

Place the two cars on a long, level piece of plastic track so that the magnets will repel as the cars approach one another, as shown in Figure 20. With one car at rest in the middle of the track, place the other car near the end of the track and give it a push so that it approaches the car at rest. What happens as the moving car approaches the car at rest? Repeat the

Bump but Do Not Touch

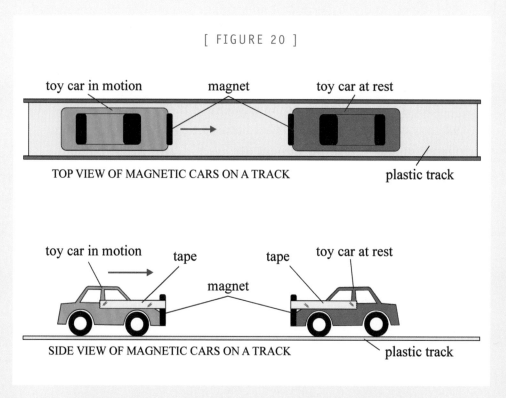

[FIGURE 20]

toy car in motion   magnet   toy car at rest

TOP VIEW OF MAGNETIC CARS ON A TRACK   plastic track

toy car in motion   tape   tape   toy car at rest

magnet

SIDE VIEW OF MAGNETIC CARS ON A TRACK   plastic track

What happens as one magnetic car approaches the other?

experiment several times and closely observe what happens. What happens to the car that was at rest? What happens to the car that was in motion?

Switch cars (moving and stationary) and repeat the experiment. Are the results the same?

Next, prepare a piece of clay that has the same weight as one car. Hold the car in one hand so that no pressure is applied to the wheels as you gently press the lump of clay onto the top of the car with your other hand. Let the car that now weighs twice as much as the other serve as the stationary car and repeat the experiment. How do the cars behave this time? What is different about the way they interact now?

Repeat the experiment, but this time have the lighter car at rest and put the heavier car in motion. What happens this time? How does this interaction differ from the previous one?

Hold another magnet with your fingertips. How can you use the magnet to make one of the magnetic cars move away from you? How can you use the magnet to make the car come toward you?

Place a ruler beside the magnet on one of the cars. Then, with your hand, move a single magnet toward the car so that the car is repelled by the magnet in your hand. At what distance between the two magnets does the car just begin to move? Repeat the experiment several times to be sure your results are consistent. Next, repeat the experiment with a stack of two magnets in your hand. At what distance between the magnets does the car start to move now? Try the experiment again with a stack of three magnets in your hand. Does the number of individual magnets in a stack of magnets affect the strength of the magnet as a whole? How do you know?

Science Fair Project Idea

Early in the nineteenth century, scientists thought that electricity and magnetism were independent phenomena, even though both exhibited forces of attraction and repulsion. How did experiments performed by Hans Christian Oersted and Michael Faraday show that electricity and magnetism are related? You might begin your research in a science encyclopedia, and go on to books about electricity and magnetism.

Under adult supervision, carry out some of the experiments performed by Oersted and Faraday that show how electricity and magnetism are related.

Materials:

- an adult
- 2 large (more than 20 cm [8 in] long) toy trucks that have wheels with very little friction
- 2 hacksaw blades
- duct tape
- smooth level surface
- weights, such as stones, small bags of sand or pebbles, or similar items that can be used to add weight to the trucks
- balance to weigh trucks
- chair or some other heavy stationary object

The previous experiment can be done in a different way without magnets. You will need two similar large toy trucks that have wheels with very little friction and two hacksaw blades. **Ask an adult** to help you use duct tape to fasten a hacksaw blade to the front of each truck, as shown in Figure 21. Be sure the two hacksaw blades are level and at the same height so that they will meet and bend as the trucks collide.

With one truck at rest on a smooth level surface, give the other truck a push so that the springlike hacksaw blades (not the trucks) meet and bend.

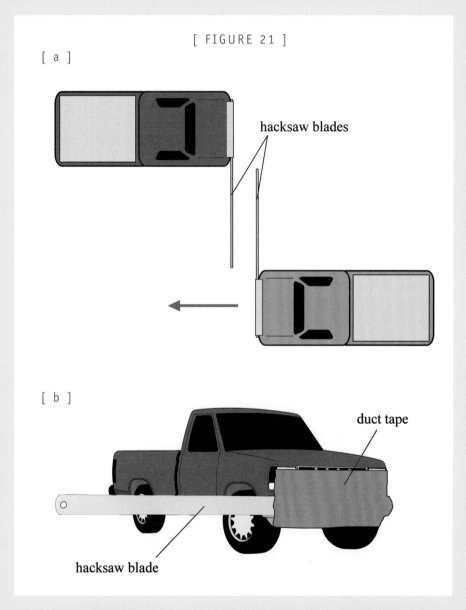

[FIGURE 21]

[a]

hacksaw blades

[b]

duct tape

hacksaw blade

21 a) A top view of toy trucks with attached hacksaw blades just before they collide. b) A view of the toy truck to show how the hacksaw blade is attached.

If the trucks turn sideways when they collide, you will have to add some weight to each truck. You could add stones, small bags of sand or pebbles, or whatever you can improvise. Be sure both trucks have the same weight.

When you are sure the trucks will not turn sideways as they collide, you are ready to begin the experiment. Place the two trucks about 30 cm (1 ft) apart on a long, level surface where the hacksaw blades can meet. With one truck at rest, give the other truck a push so that it approaches the car at rest. What happens as the hacksaw blades collide? Repeat the experiment several times and observe what happens closely. What happens to the car that was at rest? What happens to the car that was in motion?

Switch cars (moving and stationary) and repeat the experiment. Are the results the same?

Next, add weight to one truck so it is approximately twice as heavy as the other. Let the heavier truck be the stationary one as you repeat the experiment. How do the trucks behave this time? What is different about the way they interact now?

Repeat the experiment with the lighter truck at rest. What happens this time? How does this interaction differ from the previous one (Experiment 4.6)? How are they similar?

DISAPPEARING ENERGY?

Watch closely as the hacksaw blades attached to the two trucks of equal weight collide. The moving truck has kinetic energy (energy of motion) as it approaches the stationary truck. After the moving truck loses its energy and comes to rest, the truck that was stationary moves away with most of the kinetic energy. But during the time they are interacting, some kinetic energy is lost. Is the energy really lost, or is it changed to some other form of energy?

Possibly the lost kinetic energy is stored in the bent, springy hacksaw blades. You can carry out a simple experiment to find out. Push the two trucks close together so as to bend the hacksaw blades, as shown in Figure 22. This is what happens to the blades when the trucks interact.

[FIGURE 22]

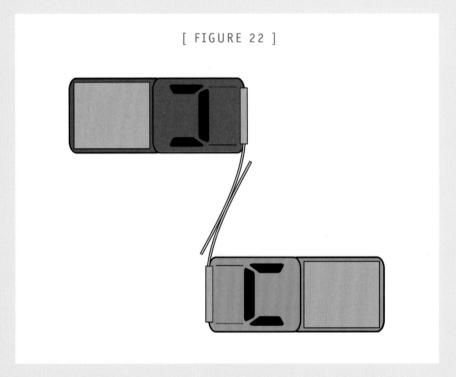

A top view shows two toy trucks pushed together so that the hacksaw blades are bent. What happens when the trucks are released?

Now, suddenly release the trucks at the same time. What happens? Is there any evidence of kinetic energy when you release the trucks?

There is another way to see this change of kinetic energy to potential energy back to kinetic energy. Push one of the trucks so that its hacksaw blade hits a fixed object such as the leg of a chair on which someone is sitting. What happens? Does the truck, at some point during the collision, lose all of its kinetic energy? How do you know? Does it regain much of its kinetic energy after the collision? What is different about its motion after the collision as compared to its motion before the collision?

Science Fair Project Idea

What is the law of conservation of energy? What evidence is there to support the law?

4.8 Ride Safely on a Toy Car

Materials:

- small doll
- wide board
- books or wooden blocks
- large toy car or truck, or roller skate
- smooth, level surface, such as a driveway, sidewalk, or concrete floor
- brick
- strong, wide rubber bands

In most states the law requires that you wear a seat belt when you ride in a car. This experiment will help you to understand why seat belts help to reduce traffic fatalities.

A doll can be used to represent an automobile passenger. Rest one end of a thin, wide board on some books or wooden blocks to make an incline. Place a large toy car or truck, or roller skate, at the top of the incline and let it roll down the "hill" and onto a smooth, level surface.

Place a brick or some other heavy object a short distance beyond the end of the incline. Place the doll on the car, truck, or roller skate and let the vehicle with its "passenger" roll down the incline and collide with the brick. What happens to the vehicle? What happens to the "passenger" when the vehicle crashes into the brick?

Repeat the experiment, but this time fasten the doll to the vehicle with strong, wide rubber bands, as shown in Figure 23. What happens to the passenger during the collision this time? Based on the results of this experiment, why do you think seat belts reduce deaths caused by traffic accidents?

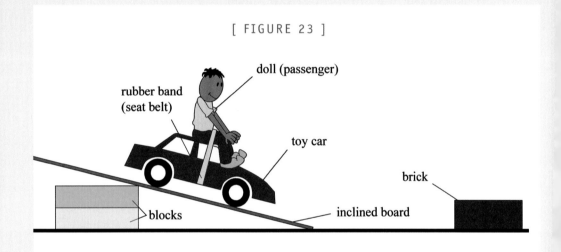

[FIGURE 23]

In this experiment, the "passenger" is firmly attached to the vehicle with a rubber band that acts like a seat belt.

Science Fair Project Ideas

- How do Newton's first and second laws of motion apply to automobile accidents?
- Design and carry out an experiment to show how the barrels of sand placed in front of concrete barriers at many exits from superhighways reduce the damage and loss of life that would occur if the cars collided with the concrete.

Chapter 5

Forces and the Bicycle

BY NOW, YOU ARE PROBABLY VERY FAMILIAR WITH NEWTON'S LAWS OF MOTION. In this chapter, we will apply these laws to bicycling. You know that the first part of Newton's first law of motion tells us that a body in motion maintains its speed and direction of motion. It would be an easy ride indeed if all you had to do was get started on your bike and let Newton's first law take over. You would just continue to roll along at the same speed and in the same direction without ever having to pedal.

The second part of Newton's first law states that a body in motion maintains its speed and direction of motion *unless acted upon by an unbalanced force*. Those forces that act on you, me, and everything else are always with us. We try to pedal up a steep hill and the force of gravity causes our speed to decrease. If we are going down the hill, gravity pulls on us and our speed increases, even when we do not pedal.

Newton's second law describes what happens when an unbalanced force does act. It tells us that when such a force acts on an object, that object accelerates; that is, its velocity changes. The speed may increase or decrease, or the object may change direction, depending on which way the force pushes or pulls the object. When you are going uphill, for example, the force of gravity acts to reduce your speed; the same force acts to increase your speed if you are going downhill. Furthermore, this second law tells us that the acceleration is proportional to the total force that acts on the object and inversely proportional to the mass of the object. This means that if the force doubles, the acceleration doubles. If the amount of matter (which is what mass is) in the object doubles, the acceleration is halved.

In an ideal world, if you gave an object a small push, it would accelerate while you pushed on it. Once you stopped pushing, it would continue to move in the same direction at a constant speed until another force acted on it. In the real world, there is a type of force that almost always opposes motion. You probably already know from Chapter 1 that force is friction.

Even though friction opposes motion, we cannot move without it. If you tried to walk or ride your bike on a frictionless surface, you could not move. You may have experienced something very close to a frictionless surface if you have tried to walk on very smooth, slightly wet ice. It is only because we are able to push back against the ground with our feet or with a bicycle's tire that we can move forward. The fact that we move forward only when we push back is explained by Newton's third law of motion. The third law states, "To every action there is an equal and opposite reaction." This means, for example, that when you push back against the earth with your foot, the earth exerts an equal force forward on your foot.

In the next experiment, you will find the force of friction that opposes the motion of your bicycle.

5.1 Friction and Your Bicycle

Materials:

- spring scale
- bicycle
- heavy string
- friend
- different smooth, level surfaces such as macadam, concrete, dirt, gravel, grass, and sand
- heavy person
- light person
- tire gauge
- bicycle tire pump
- graph paper
- pencil

Spring scales, like the one you may have used in previous experiments (see Figure 24a), can be used to measure forces. Since friction is a force, we should be able to measure it with a spring scale.

To find the frictional force that opposes the motion of your bicycle, begin by tying a heavy string around the front part of your bike's frame. Attach the string to a spring scale. You will use the scale to pull the bike forward at a slow but steady speed along a smooth, level surface. As long as the speed is constant, the force you exert will be just enough to overcome friction. Have a friend keep your bicycle upright without pushing it or pressing down on it, while you pull the bike forward, as shown in Figure 24b. According to the spring scale, what is the frictional force that opposes the motion of your riderless bicycle? What happens to the bike's speed when you pull with a force greater than the force of friction?

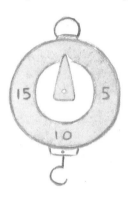

[FIGURE 24b]

24 a) Any of these spring scales can be used to measure forces.
b) How much friction is there between your bike's tires and
the surface over which it rolls?

FRICTION ON DIFFERENT SURFACES

Repeat the experiment with the bike on different level surfaces. You might try it on macadam (blacktop pavement), concrete, dirt, gravel, grass, sand, and other surfaces. Is the frictional force that acts on your bicycle related to the surface over which the bike rolls? If it is, on which surface is the friction greatest? On which surface is friction the least?

FRICTION AND WEIGHT

How does weight affect the frictional force on your bicycle? To find out, have a friend sit on the bike as you pull it with a spring scale along a smooth, level surface at a small but constant speed. Is the force the same, greater, or less than it was when you pulled the bike without anyone on it?

Suppose someone much heavier than your friend sits on the bike while you pull it with a spring scale. Do you think the friction between the bike and the surface over which it rolls will be the same as, greater than, or less than it was when your lighter friend was on the bike? Try it. Were you right? Why must you do this experiment on the same surface you used when you pulled your first friend along?

Suppose someone who weighs much less than your first friend sits on the bike while you pull it with the spring scale. Do you think the friction between the bike and the surface over which it rolls will be the same as, greater than, or less than it was when your friend was on the bike? Try it. Were you right?

Suppose you pull your bike, with your first friend on board, along differ-ent surfaces, such as those you tried before (macadam, concrete, dirt, gravel, grass, sand, etc.). Do you think the frictional force will be different on different surfaces? If you do, try to predict what those forces will be. Were your predictions close to the actual force measurements you made?

FRICTION AND TIRE PRESSURE

Does the pressure of the tires affect the force of friction? To find out, ask a friend to sit on your bicycle. Then use a spring scale to pull him or her

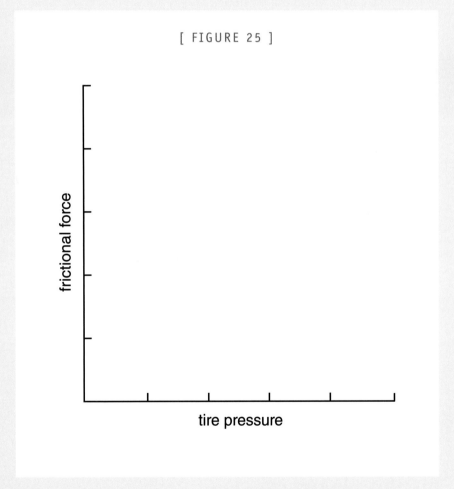

[FIGURE 25]

frictional force

tire pressure

Does tire pressure affect the frictional force acting on your bicycle?

along a smooth, level surface at a small but steady speed. With what force do you have to pull the bike and your friend to overcome friction? Next, use a tire gauge to measure the air pressure in the tires. Reduce that pressure to about 4/5 of what it was and repeat the experiment. Do you find any change in the frictional force acting on the bicycle?

Repeat the experiment at about 3/5, then 2/5, and finally 1/5 of its original pressure. Using axes like those shown in Figure 25, plot a graph of the frictional force on your bicycle versus the air pressure in the tires. What do you conclude?

Finally, use a bicycle pump to reinflate your tires to the proper pressure.

 Science Fair Project Ideas

- Does the width of the tires affect the frictional force acting on the bicycle? Design and carry out an experiment to find out.
- Does the diameter of the tires affect the frictional force acting on the bicycle? Design and carry out an experiment to find out.
- In Experiment 5.1 you measured rolling friction. The wheel was free to turn as you pulled the bike along a level surface. Design and carry out an experiment to measure sliding friction; that is, to find the force needed to slide the bicycle forward at a steady speed when the wheels cannot turn. How does sliding friction compare with rolling friction?

5.2 Bicycle Wheels and Ball Bearings

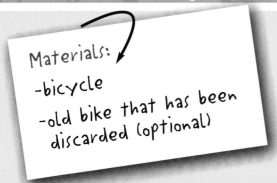

Materials:

-bicycle
-old bike that has been discarded (optional)

In this experiment you will see how important ball bearings are in your bicycle.

Turn your bicycle upside down so that it rests on the handlebars and seat. Then give the front wheel a pull to make it spin. Notice how easily it turns. You may also notice that it continues to turn for a long time! Does this make you think of one of Newton's laws?

The reason your bicycle wheel spins so easily is because its axle turns on ball bearings. For the same reason, your bike pedals turn very easily, especially if you remove the chain from the front sprocket. The axle connecting the cranks that attach to the pedals turn on ball bearings.

If you can find an old bike that has been discarded, you might like to take the wheels, the cranks, and front sprocket apart so that you can see the ball bearings that reduce friction to a minimum. Another approach might be to visit a bicycle repair shop. You could ask the owner for permission to watch while a repair is done on a part that exposes the ball bearings.

How many ball bearings do you see? How large are they? On what do the bearings turn?

5.3 How Does Pedal Position Affect the Force?

Materials:

- bicycle
- string, fishing line, or fine wire
- weight
- spring scale
- partner
- boards

Normally, the force that makes your bicycle move comes from you pushing on the pedals. But as you know, pushing down on a pedal at some positions has little or no effect on the bicycle. How is the force that drives a bicycle forward related to the position of the pedal when you push on it?

To find out, you can use string, fishing line, or fine wire to hang a known weight on a pedal as shown in Figure 26a. Attach a spring scale to the bicycle frame. Hold the scale in a horizontal position (see Figure 26b). It will enable you to measure the forward force on the bicycle when the weighted pedal is at different angles. Ask a partner to keep the bicycle upright, being careful not to exert any force that would move the bike forward or backward. If the weight hangs so far below the pedal that it strikes the ground at certain angles, you can place the front and rear wheels on stacks of boards. In that way, the weight can hang well below the pedal without touching the ground even at its lowest point.

At what position does the pedal produce the largest forward force on the bicycle? At what position or positions does the pedal exert no forward force on the bicycle?

FROM COASTER BRAKES TO MACHINES, FORCES, AND WORK

Did you know that the coaster brakes that were found on most bicycles in the middle of the twentieth century were inefficient? To see why that is true, you need to first examine what is meant by mechanical advantage, work, and efficiency.

[FIGURE 26a]

[FIGURE 26b]

26 a) Hang a weight from the pedal. The pedal can then be set at
different angles. b) Use a spring scale to measure the forward
force on the bicycle when the weighted pedal is at various
positions. Both wheels can be elevated to prevent the weight
from touching the ground.

A bicycle is a complex machine that is made of many simple machines. There are six basic types of machines: the inclined plane, the wedge, the lever, the wheel and axle, the pulley, and the screw. Examples of these simple machines are shown in Figure 27.

Humans invented machines to make their work easier or to change the direction of a force used to do work. For example, the pulley in Figure 27f allows the worker to lift the weight by pulling down rather than risking a back injury by bending over to lift it. A lever, such as the wheelbarrow shown in Figure 27d, allows a person to apply a larger or smaller force to an object than the one he or she could exert at another point on the lever.

You may be wondering how a machine can magnify a force. You might be thinking, "Doesn't that break some kind of scientific law, such as conservation of energy?" The answer is no! The reason is that the work the person does (the energy he or she provides) is always more than the work output of the machine. To see why, look at the boy pushing down on the lever in Figure 28. He exerts a force of 100 newtons (22.5 lbs) at a distance of 1.0 m from the fulcrum in order to lift a weight of 400 newtons (90 lbs) that is 0.25 m from the fulcrum. The boy's mechanical advantage is 4.0 because the output force (the force that lifts the weight) of 400 N is 4 times greater than the input force of 100 N that the boy exerts. By definition,

$$\text{mechanical advantage} = \frac{\text{output force}}{\text{input force}}$$

But the work done on something is defined as the force acting on the object times the distance through which the force acts. The boy has to push downward through a distance of 0.4 m in order to raise the weight 0.1 m. Consequently, the work done by the boy (the work input) is

100 N × 0.4 m = 40 N-m or 40 joules
(One joule [J] is equal to one newton-meter.)

The work done on the weight (the work output) is

400 N × 0.1 m = 40 N-m or 40 J

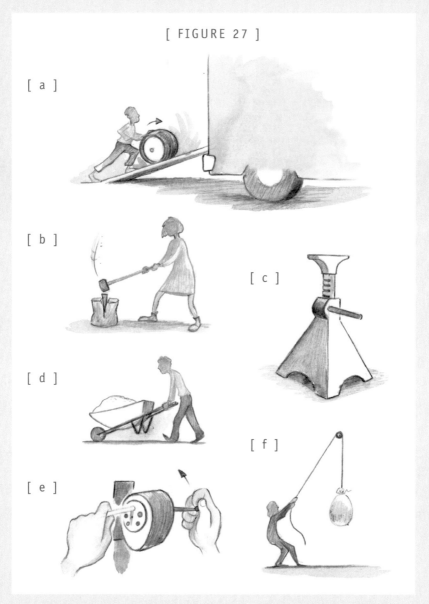

[FIGURE 27]

[a]

[b]

[c]

[d]

[f]

[e]

27. Examples of simple machines: a) inclined plane; b) wedge;
c) screw; d) levers; e) wheel and axle; f) pulley. How many simple
machines can you find on your bicycle?

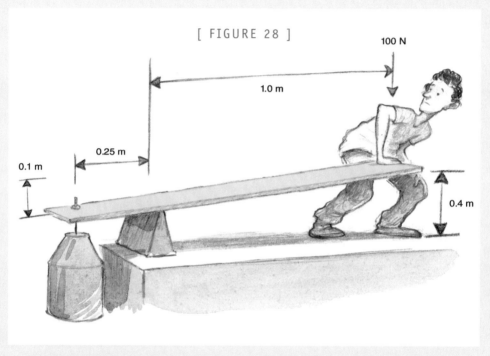

[FIGURE 28]

100 N

1.0 m

0.25 m

0.1 m

0.4 m

To lift a 400-N weight 0.1 m, the boy exerts a force of 100 N through a distance of 0.4 m. The work done on the weight is 400 N × 0.1 m = 40 J. How much work does the boy do?

Actually, the work done by the boy will be more than the work done on the weight because the boy has to overcome frictional forces between the lever and the fulcrum that oppose the force he exerts. For example, the force he exerts might actually be 104 N. If that were the case, the work input would exceed the work output by 1.6 J because

$$104 \text{ N} \times 0.4 \text{ m} = 41.6 \text{ J, and } 41.6 \text{ J} - 40 \text{ J} = 1.6 \text{ J}$$

Efficiency is defined as the ratio of work output to work input. In this case, the efficiency would be

$$\frac{\text{work output}}{\text{work input}} = \frac{40 \text{ J}}{41.6 \text{ J}} = 0.96 \text{ or } 96 \text{ \%}$$

So what does all of this have to do with coaster brakes and efficiency? The next experiment should help you answer that question.

5.4 Bikes, Brakes, and Levers

Materials:
- bicycle with a coaster brake
- bicycle with hand brakes
- 2 spring scales
- heavy object such as dumbbell weight, doorstop, wedge, or brick
- heavy duty tape (such as duct tape)
- string
- ruler
- partner

Bikes that have balloon tires and a single gear on both front and rear sprockets usually have a coaster brake. You may notice that the rear hub on these bikes is larger than the hub on most bicycles. The reason is that there is a brake mechanism inside the hub that hinders (slows down) the rotation of the axle. To make the coaster brake work, a rider pushes backward on the pedals. The chain, in turn, pushes back on the rear sprocket, which causes the brake inside the hub to push against the axle and reduce the bike's speed.

You can compare a coaster brake with the hand-operated brakes on most multi-geared bicycles. In hand-operated brakes, a system of levers connected by strong wires squeezes hard rubber brake pads against the rims of the bike's wheels. There is a brake for both the rear wheel and the front wheel.

There are several ways to compare these two braking systems. One way is to try to turn the rear wheel of a bike with a coaster brake while the brake is on. Then try to turn the wheel of a multispeed bike while the hand brake squeezes the brake pads firmly against the wheel's rim. In which case is the wheel easier to turn? Can you explain why?

The major difference between these two braking systems is the place where the force is applied to the wheel. The coaster brake acts on the axle of the wheel. With the multispeed bike, the braking force acts on the rim of the wheel. You can feel the difference between these two braking mechanisms. First, grasp the spokes of a bicycle wheel close to the hub with your right hand. Grasp the tire of the same wheel with your left hand. Now try to prevent the wheel from turning with your right hand while you turn the wheel slowly with your left hand. Can you prevent the wheel from turning? (Be careful not to bend the spokes.)

Repeat the experiment, but this time grasp the *rim* of the wheel with your right hand. You will find it much easier to stop the turning action of your left hand. About how much harder do you have to pull to turn the wheel when your braking hand (right hand) is on the rim instead of on the axle?

For a more quantitative experiment, use a spring scale to find the weight of a heavy object such as a dumbbell weight (wedge, doorstop, or brick). Tape the heavy object to the tire of an inverted bicycle as shown in Figure 29. Tape a string to the tire on the opposite side of the wheel. Using a spring scale, measure the force on the spring needed to balance the wheel and keep it from turning. How does the force compare with the weight of the object?

Next, measure the force needed to keep the wheel from turning when the scale is connected to a spoke near the hub of the wheel (see Figure 29). Finally, measure the force needed to keep the wheel from turning when the scale is attached to a spoke near the rim of the wheel.

As you have found, forces applied at different points along the radius of a wheel behave much like those acting on a lever. To see this more directly, attach strings to spokes on opposite sides of the wheel. Place one string 20 cm (8 in) from the center of the wheel. Place the other string 10 cm (4 in) from the center on the opposite side of the wheel, as shown in Figure 30. Attach spring scales to the strings. Pull on one spring while a friend pulls on the other so that the wheel does not turn. You will find that the force

[FIGURE 29]

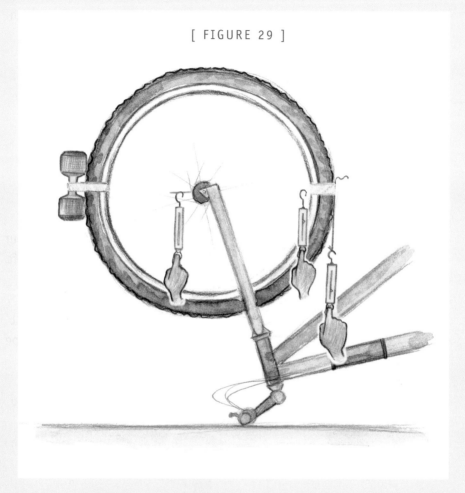

A coaster brake acts on a wheel's axle. Why is it better to have a brake that acts on the rim of the wheel?

20 cm (8 in) from the center is just half as large as the balancing force 10 cm (4 in) from the center. What mechanical advantage does this setup provide? You can make a similar model with a pin, drinking straws, and paper clips in Experiment 2.3 (see Figure 7).

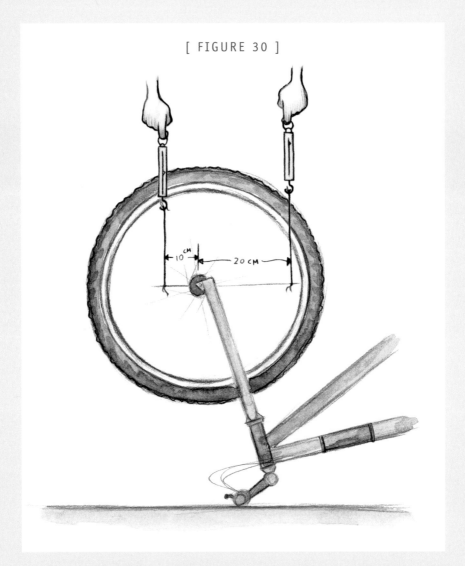

[FIGURE 30]

A bicycle wheel, which is a simple wheel and axle, can serve as a machine.

5.5 A Bicycle-Wheel Centrifuge

Materials:
- fine starch or flour
- clear plastic vial or pill bottle with a cap (Do not use glass.)
- water
- bicycle
- heavy blocks to support bicycle on its side
- tape
- muddy water
- cooking oil in soapy water

A centrifuge is a device used by chemists to make insoluble particles settle out of solution faster. A test tube containing a mixture of solid and liquid is placed in the centrifuge. The centrifuge then spins around at high speed. The bottom of the test tube is farthest from the center of the machine so that the heavier solid particles, which are "thrown" outward by the spinning motion, wind up at the bottom of the tube.

You can prepare a mixture of a liquid and an insoluble solid by adding some fine starch or flour to a clear plastic vial or pill bottle that is three-quarters filled with water. Put a cap on the container and shake it. Notice how slowly the particles settle to the bottom of the vial.

To increase the rate at which the solid separates from the liquid, you can turn your bicycle wheel into a centrifuge. Put the bike in its highest gear, turn it on its side, and support it on some heavy blocks. Then tape the capped vial to spokes near the rim of the wheel, as shown in Figure 31. Use a pedal to spin the wheel at high speed for about 10 seconds. Then stop the wheel and look at the vial. What has happened to the starch or flour particles?

Can you use your bicycle centrifuge to turn muddy water clear? Can you use it to separate cooking oil mixed with soapy water? What force is at work in a centrifuge?

[FIGURE 31]

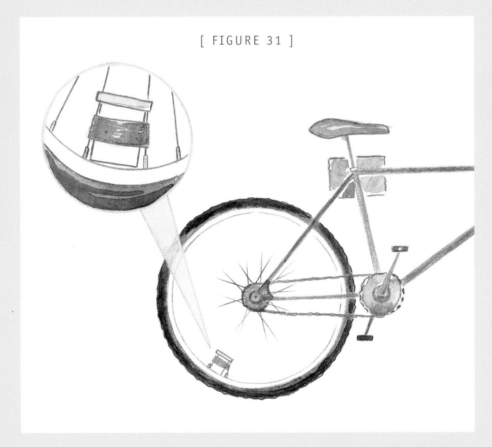

A bicycle wheel can be used as a centrifuge.

FURTHER READING

Books

Bochinski, Julianne Blair. *The Complete Workbook for Science Fair Projects.* Hoboken, N.J.: John Wiley and Sons, Inc., 2005.

Buttitta, Hope. *It's Not Magic, It's Science!: 50 Science Tricks that Mystify, Dazzle, and Astound!* New York: Lark Books, A Division of Sterling Publishing Co., Inc., 2005.

Hammond, Richard. *Can You Feel the Force?* New York: DK Publishing, 2006.

Moorman, Thomas. *How to Make Your Science Project Scientific, Revised Edition.* New York: John Wiley & Sons, Inc., 2002.

Pentland, Peter and Pennie Stoyles. *Toy and Game Science.* Broomall, Pa.: Chelsea House Publishers, 2003.

Rosinsky, Natalie M. *Sir Isaac Newton: Brilliant Mathematician and Scientist.* Minneapolis, Minn.: Compass Point Books, 2008.

Silverstein, Alvin , Virginia Silverstein, and Laura Silverstein Nunn. *Forces and Motion.* Minneapolis, Minn.: Twenty-First Century Books, 2009.

Internet Addresses

Funburst Media, LLC. *Funology. The Science of Having Fun.* 1999–2005.
<http://www.funology.com/laboratory/>

New York Hall of Science. *Try Science.* 1999-2008.
<http://www.tryscience.org/experiments/experiments_home.html>

Science Hound. *All Science Fair Projects.com.* 2006.
<http://www.all-science-fair-projects.com/>

INDEX